W9-BEV-801

PHILOSOPHICAL ANALYSIS

PHILOSOPHICAL ANALYSIS:

An Introduction to Its Language and Techniques

Third Edition

Samuel Gorovitz, *University of Maryland*

Merrill Hintikka, *Florida State University*

Donald Provence, *San Francisco State University*

Ron G. Williams, *Colorado State University*

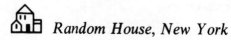 *Random House, New York*

Third Edition
9876
Copyright © 1963 by Samuel Gorovitz and Ron G. Williams
Copyright © 1965, 1969, 1979 by Random House, Inc.

All rights reserved under International and Pan-American Copyright Conventions. No part of this book may be reproduced in any form or by any means, electronic or mechanical, including photocopying, without permission in writing from the publisher. All inquiries should be addressed to Random House, Inc., 201 East 50th Street, New York, N.Y. 10022. Published in the United States by Random House, Inc., and simultaneously in Canada by Random House of Canada Limited, Totonto.

Library of Congress Cataloging in Publication Data

Gorovitz, Samuel.
    Philosophical analysis.

    Bibliography: p.
    Includes index.
    1. Analysis (Philosophy) I. Title.
B808.5.G6   1979   149'.94   78-25661
ISBN 0-394-32284-3

MANUFACTURED IN THE UNITED STATES OF AMERICA

Preface to the Third Edition

In preparing extensive revisions to the second edition, we have continued to hold to the aims expressed in the preface to the first edition. Primary among these was to provide a concise introduction to the language of contemporary philosophy that would enable a beginning student then to study some basic philosophical problems in depth. We have been guided by the very helpful suggestions of students and colleagues who have used the book and also by some of the main directions that philosophic inquiry in the analytic tradition has taken in the years since the second edition appeared.

Chapter I, which introduces some of the formal tools of philosophy, has been extensively revised with an increased emphasis on enabling the student to understand sentences presented in a symbolic notation that he or she may encounter in beginning the study of philosophy. In revising and expanding the discussion of the truth conditions of such sentences, we have assumed that to know in what circumstances or under what conditions a sentence would be true is to go a long way toward understanding it. Discussion of the concepts of validity and invalidity has been extensively revised, but its aim remains to increase and sharpen a student's understanding of what it is for an argument to be valid and for an argument to be invalid. As in earlier editions, no attempt has been made to provide the student with the syntactic skills used in constructing demonstrations of validity. Chapters IV and V have also been extensively revised in light of some of the recent uses to which philosophers have put the ideas introduced there. Both chapter titles have been changed to reflect the present emphasis of the discussions. Many other sections have been revised to introduce new material as well as to amplify the old.

Exercises too have been revised, and answers or partial answers have been included for some of the exercises. An asterisk (*) before an exercise indicates that a solution or a partial solution is to be found at the back of the book.

Thanks are due to many colleagues who have shared with us their experiences when using the earlier editions in their classes and when advising prospective students in philosophy. Their suggestions have been most helpful in the revisions we have made. Particular thanks are due to Professors David Henson and Nicholas Smith, whose careful and detailed reviews and constructive suggestions have resulted in changes in emphasis as well as in content. We are grateful to Jane Cullen of Random House, who has been the impetus behind the third edition and whose patience and encouragement have sustained the project. Our debt to Professor Jaakko Hintikka extends far beyond the power of thanks to repay; his contributions ranged from authorship of some sections to insightful and constructive critique of others, and eventually to the typing of some parts of the manuscript! Without his efforts there would be no third edition.

Preface to the Second Edition

In revising the first edition, we have given particular attention to the logical notions introduced in the first three chapters and to the notation used to develop them. We have introduced several changes designed to make our remarks clearer and more precise. Several other sections have been revised in order to add new material or elucidate the old, and minor changes are widespread throughout the book. Nevertheless, we have held to the original aims expressed in the preface to the first edition and the introduction—especially to the conviction that the book is best viewed as a starting point and not as a definitive handbook.

Exercises have been added to most chapters to provide the student with opportunity for practice in using the material presented.

We have profited from discussion and correspondence with many colleagues whose useful suggestions for improvement have aided us in making revisions. Particular thanks go to Professors Nino Cocchiarella and Rolf Sartorius, and to Mr. William Thomas, for valuable suggestions which have resulted in many of the changes and corrections in this edition.

Preface to the First Edition

Students beginning the study of history, literature, or physics have for the most part a roughly accurate idea of the nature of the subject matter they are about to confront. So it is with most fields. But students beginning the study of analytic philosophy have in general no idea at all what sort of discipline they are about to encounter. This lack of knowledge presents the instructor with an additional burden—one which is not easy to overcome. For the question of the nature of philosophy is itself a philosophical issue, which can be handled properly only when the students have—or perhaps are in the process of developing—some competence in philosophy. It is in the interest of advancing the development of such competence that this book was written.

The book was conceived during the course of an informal seminar on the teaching of philosophy organized by a group of Stanford graduate students. Part of the purpose of this seminar was to develop a rather detailed syllabus for the kind of introductory philosophy course that the members of the group believed they would like to teach. The consensus was that a beginning student should be given the opportunity to study a few basic philosophical problems in depth. It was decided that treatment of a few problems in depth could best be accomplished if the student were first given a concise introduction to the language of modern philosophy. No adequate written material for such an introduction was available.

This book is thus aimed at what the authors consider to be a specific need. We intend the book to provide the materials for a program of familiarization with the language and techniques of analytic philosophy, for students who have had no prior acquaintance with the discipline.

No attempt has been made to write a comprehensive survey of any sort. The topics that are included in this volume were chosen as being most relevant to the type of problem the authors wish to treat in their own courses. However, most of the topics discussed are so basic to modern philosophical analysis that they should be relevant to many different types of courses. In addition, we have attempted to include material that will help the student avoid what, in our experience, are the mistakes most commonly made by beginning students in philosophy.

This book provides no final word and is no substitute for solid philosophical inquiry. Its purpose will be defeated if it is viewed as a compendium of philosophical method. Moreover, there is a serious danger inherent in the very nature of this book; any compact presentation of techniques and distinctions can, merely by its existence, give the impression that the problems of the discipline in question can be met simply by drawing upon a previously developed arsenal of procedures. Yet any such impression of philosophical inquiry is grossly in error. In fact, the distinctions and techniques described here, like all those in philosophy, arose out of confrontation with substantive issues and were developed in the light of new problems. Yet to justify the distinctions we discuss by presenting an historical account of their development would defeat the purpose for which the book was conceived. We have, therefore, tried to motivate the development of the material in a natural way, but the major task in this respect lies in the hands of the instructor.

The various sections of the book are, insofar as possible, independent of one another. Where there is dependence, the relevant sections are cited. Thus, sections may be omitted or used in a different sequence at the option of the instructor.

The authors wish to acknowledge their indebtedness to the Philosophy Department at Stanford University for encouragement, advice, and material support in connection with this project. We wish also to thank the other members of the seminar, Marcia Muelder Eaton, Hugh Petrie, Terry Parsons, David Howell, and John Wallace, for their help in planning this book and for their criticisms of it. Michael Rohr was very helpful in the preparation of the bibliography. Professor Vere Chappell, as the publisher's advisor, provided valuable encouragement and evaluation throughout. Finally, our thanks are due to the many people in various fields who have provided constructive suggestions for the improvement of the manuscript.

Contents

Introduction

Philosophy is a discipline relatively free of technical language and specialized methods. Whereas the problems of modern physics, for example, can be appreciated only by those trained in advanced mathematics and experimental techniques, many of the most fundamental problems of philosophy can be stated in rather simple terms.

There are, however, certain concepts that find their primary use in philosophical discourse, and there are certain techniques—particularly those of modern logic—that are commonly employed by philosophers. This book is designed to acquaint beginning students in philosophy with the most basic of these concepts and methods. A mastery of the material presented here should enable the student to progress more rapidly in the study of philosophy and to treat on a deeper level the philosophical questions he encounters. Such mastery can, of course, be gained only by a careful reading and rereading of the sections that follow.

The authors have attempted to give an impartial presentation of certain key terms and procedures—that is, a presentation that does not express a particular philosophical position. But this attempt is bound to fail, at least at some points, because virtually no interesting discussion of a basic concept is noncontroversial, nor does any method have the approval of all philosophers. Therefore, we cannot overemphasize the point that this book does not provide any final word on philosophical method. To treat the book as a philosophical dictionary, or as an authoritative discourse on methods of analysis, can lead only to trouble. No list of techniques is a substitute for careful analysis and uninhibited thinking. Hence, the intended use of this book is as a starting point for a painstaking examination of the problems of philosophy—an examination which, if pursued with diligence, will surely lead to a reappraisal of the material presented here.

PHILOSOPHICAL ANALYSIS

I

Elementary Logic

1. Introduction

The study of logic has, for over 2000 years, engaged the interest of both those who wish to gain practical advantage from a knowledge of the principles of reasoning and those who pursue the subject for its own sake. The practical benefits of this study are undeniable. Those with an interest in increasing, organizing, or using knowledge have turned to logic—from the early Greek philosophers to the men from many fields who together developed modern computer science on the basis of their knowledge of formal logic. Moreover, logic, as it develops, becomes an increasingly important and intriguing theoretical discipline. By no means a static 'body of knowledge' that exists to be learned and used, logic is a viable and creative field. Its study is an arena for creative human endeavor. The goal of logic is stable, but means for attaining that goal are being expanded and new ones formulated.

The study of logic provides a means of facilitating the attempt to develop well-argued positions and to evaluate critically the positions espoused by others. The material that follows is not designed to give the reader mastery of the techniques of formal logic. Rather, it is aimed at facilitating communication—at enabling the reader to understand some of the uses of logic which he or she will come across, in the classroom or in the literature, when beginning the study of a contemporary analytical approach to philosophical problems.

The goal of logic, which we said above was a stable one, is the preservation of truth. Before continuing a discussion of this goal, it will be helpful to distinguish conclusive from inconclusive reasoning. Conclusive reasoning *guarantees* that the goal of logic has been reached. That is, it guarantees that in the process of reasoning there has not been a passage from what is true to what is false. The study of conclusive reasoning is usually called *deductive* logic. Some reasoning, though good, is inconclusive because the information contained in the conclusion goes beyond that contained in the grounds for the conclusion. For example:

(1) Each of the twenty cows inoculated with Smith's vaccine promptly died.
(2) (Therefore) Smith's vaccine is fatal to all cows.

Here it is possible that the grounds stated in (1) are true while the conclusion drawn in (2) is false; the truth of (1) does not guarantee the truth of (2).

The study of good reasoning of this sort has usually been included in what is called *inductive* logic. While the preservation of truth may not be guaranteed in inductive reasoning, this goal remains an important principle in the evaluation of inductive reasoning and of principles of inductive logic. The analysis of inductive arguments is complex indeed and goes far beyond the scope of our present concerns. In our subsequent discussion we shall restrict our attention to conclusive reasoning.

In distinguishing between conclusive and inconclusive reasoning, we utilized the idea of passage from grounds to conclusions. We may consider logic to be an analysis of the structure of reasoning. Although we do not maintain that all reasoning need be linguistic, it is convenient for the purposes at hand to give a linguistic formulation of these ideas of grounds, passage, and conclusion. Let us think then of a single instance of reasoning as an *argument*. An argument is a set of declarative sentences, one of which is claimed to follow from the others and is identified as the *conclusion*. The remaining sentences, which are offered as grounds for the conclusion, are called *premises*.

The most basic mark of quality for an argument is validity. An argument is *valid* when it is not possible for all its premises to be true while the conclusion is false. Obviously such arguments guarantee the preservation of truth in that one cannot start from premises, all of which are true, and yet end with a conclusion which is false. Notice, however, that the preservation of truth does not require that all truths explicit in the premises have been preserved. Typically the conclusion of a valid argument will not contain all the information that is guaranteed by the grounds.

As a goal, the preservation of truth is a kind of quality control on reasoning. But even strict adherence to that goal will not alone guarantee that the conclusions which are the products of our reasoning are true. For even flawless reasoning *can* lead to a false conclusion if it begins from grounds which include a false premise. For this reason it is useful to notice a distinction between arguments that exhibit good reasoning and arguments that not only exhibit good reasoning but also start with true premises. Arguments of the former kind we have called valid; arguments of the latter kind we will call *sound*. That is, an argument is sound if and only if it is a valid argument having no false premise. We can thus challenge the soundness of an argument either by challenging its validity or by challenging the truth of one or more of its premises.

Usually we want our arguments to be not only valid but also sound, since when we know that an argument is sound we know that its conclusion is true. But arguments which are valid though not sound may also be useful. For example we can, when certain conditions are met, use an argument which is valid but not sound to show that a particular sentence is false. Suppose we know both that an argument is valid and that its conclusion is false. We know then that at least one of its premises is false. For if all the premises of a valid argument are true, its conclusion is true. Now suppose also that we know, of all its premises but one, that they are true. Then it must be that one premise which is false.

If it is more often the soundness of an argument than merely its validity that we seek, why can we not think of the goal of logic as extended beyond analysis of the structure of reasoning and arguments to evaluation of grounds or premises? To do so would be to include within the subject of logic not only the structure of reasoning but also absolutely everything else that can find its way into the premises of our reasoning! Against this prospect of the whole of human knowledge as the proper purview of logic, a guarantee of the preservation of truth is a modest aim indeed. But it is not a trivial one; pursuit of this goal is of value throughout the quest for knowledge.

2. Arguments, Validity, and Truth

Let us consider some examples to illustrate the general discussion above.

(1) All men are bipeds.

A (2) Edgar is a man.

(3) (Therefore) Edgar is a biped.

is an argument in which line $A(3)$ is the conclusion that is indicated to follow from lines $A(1)$ and $A(2)$. If we know $A(1)$ and $A(2)$, we can deduce that $A(3)$ is true. Lines $A(1)$ and $A(2)$ are called premises; line $A(3)$ is called the conclusion. Here the fact that a conclusion is sometimes, but not always, marked by a word such as 'therefore' or 'so' is shown by enclosing the indicator in parentheses.

Consider the following three sentences:

   (1) All women are bipeds.
B   (2) Helen is a woman.
   (3) (Therefore) Rover is a biped.

Here, too, we have an argument, which bears some resemblance to *A* in form. But this time we notice something strange. The purported conclusion, line $B(3)$, does not follow from the premises at all. Even if $B(1)$ and $B(2)$ are true, $B(3)$ is not thereby guaranteed to be true. So *B*, like *A*, is an argument; but *B*, unlike *A*, is not a good argument. Its conclusion does not follow from its premises, and we call such arguments *invalid*.

I may know that no one in San Francisco is seven feet tall and that Jean Jones is a five-foot New Yorker. Still, I can assert that if it *were* true that all San Franciscans are seven feet tall and that Jean Jones lives in San Francisco, then it would be true that Jean Jones is seven feet tall. My argument would look like this:

   (1) All San Franciscans are seven feet tall.
C   (2) Jean Jones is a San Franciscan.
   (3) (Therefore) Jean Jones is seven feet tall.

Argument *C*, like argument *A*, is valid; that is, both arguments are such that it must be that if the premises are true, the conclusion is true. The conclusion of a valid argument is a logical consequence of its premises, and the premises are said to imply or to entail the conclusion. But *C*, unlike *A*, has false premises. Thus *C* is a valid argument, but it is not sound. Argument *C* illustrates the fact that a sentence can be the conclusion of a valid argument and still be false. For, to say that a sentence is the conclusion of a valid argument is to say only that its truth is guaranteed *if* the premises of the argument are true. But consider *D*:

	(1)	All men are mortal.
D	(2)	Socrates is a man.
	(3)	(Therefore) Jean Jones is seven feet tall.

Here the conclusion clearly does not follow. Argument *D* is invalid. Yet *D*(3) is the same sentence as *C*(3). That sentence is both the conclusion of a valid argument and the conclusion of an invalid argument. It is helpful in beginning the study of philosophy to speak only of arguments, not of sentences, as being valid or invalid and to speak only of sentences as being true or false.

To illustrate further the difference between truth and validity, let us consider the following arguments:

	(1) All professional tennis players are athletes.	T	
E	(2) Billie Jean King is a professional tennis player.	T	V
	(3) Billie Jean King is an athlete.	T	
	(1) All Oakland Raiders are football players.	T	
F	(2) Ken Stabler is a football player.	T	I
	(3) Ken Stabler is an Oakland Raider.	T	

G	(1) All athletes are professional golfers.	F	
	(2) Arthur Ashe is an athlete.	T	V
	(3) Arthur Ashe is a professional golfer.	F	

H	(1) All philosophers are Greeks.	F	
	(2) Inge Broverman is a psychologist.	T	I
	(3) Inge Broverman is a Greek.	F	

I	(1) All humans are whales.	F	
	(2) All whales are mammals.	T	V
	(3) All humans are mammals.	T	

J	(1) All whales are humans.	F	
	(2) All whales are mammals.	T	I
	(3) All humans are mammals.	T	

K	(1) All humans are dogs.	F	
	(2) Lassie is a human.	F	V
	(3) Lassie is a dog.	T	

L	(1) All humans are fish.	F	
	(2) Lassie is a human.	F	I
	(3) Lassie is a dog.	T	

M	(1) All senators are Democrats.	F	
	(2) Gerald Ford is a senator.	F	V
	(3) Gerald Ford is a Democrat.	F	

N	(1) All Federal judges are Republicans.	F	
	(2) Barbara Jordan is a Republican.	F	I
	(3) Barbara Jordan is a Federal judge.	F	

.
.
.

	(1) All Republican senators are U.S. citizens.	T	
O	(2) All Democratic senators are U.S. citizens.	T	I
	(3) All Republican senators are Democratic senators.	F	

In each of these arguments, we may regard the first two sentences as premises or grounds and the third as a conclusion which is purported to follow from the premises. It is convenient to speak of the *truth value* of a sentence in referring to its truth, if the sentence is true, or to its falsity, if the sentence is false. For many of these arguments, their validity or invalidity is intuitively obvious. Since a proof of the validity or invalidity of these arguments is beyond the scope of this book, we will capitalize on the reader's intuitions in using these arguments to illustrate some important points about relations between an argument's validity or invalidity and the truth values of its premises and conclusion.

We note, for example, that E is a valid argument with true premises and a true conclusion, while F is an invalid argument although, as in the case of E, each of its premises and its conclusion are true. We can schematize this situation, as we have done to the right of the above arguments, indicating the truth value of premises and conclusion (using 'T' for 'true' and 'F' for 'false') and the validity or invalidity of each argument (using 'V' for 'valid' and 'I' for 'invalid').

Argument G is a valid argument with one false premise, one true premise, and a false conclusion. However H, while it is like G in having one false premise, one true premise, and a false conclusion, is unlike G in a most important respect: H

is an invalid argument. The pair of arguments *G* and *H* (as well as each of the pairs *E* and *F*, *I*, and *J*, *K* and *L*, *M* and *N*) illustrates that two arguments may be exactly alike in respect to the truth value of their premises and their respective conclusions while differing in an all-important respect: their validity or invalidity. This fact is not surprising if we recall that an argument is valid just in case it is *not possible* for its premises to be true while its conclusion is false.

How does *F* fare in light of this informal account of validity? Although its conclusion is in fact true, it is possible for the premises of *F* to be true and its conclusion false. Stabler could be traded to another football team, or he might play out his option and sign with a rival club. In fact, even though the conclusion of *F* is true when this page is being written, that sentence may have a different truth value when you are reading this book. Similarly, many other sentences in our example arguments may have different truth values as you read this book than they had when we indicated their truth values. The truth of the premises of *F* does not exclude these possibilities; the truth of the premises of *F* does not guarantee the truth of its conclusion. It is beyond the scope of this book to provide the reader with skills needed to *demonstrate* that the truth of the premises of *E does* guarantee the truth of its conclusion. Nonetheless, the possibility that Billie Jean King is not an athlete is excluded by the truth of the premises of *E*.

Arguments *E*, *G*, *I*, *K*, and *M* are all valid. Yet only *E*, *I*, and *K* have true conclusions. So we see that the conclusion of a valid argument may be a false sentence. A valid argument guarantees the preservation of truth in that its conclusion is true if all its premises are true. This requirement on a valid argument says nothing about the truth value of the conclusion of a valid argument with one or more false premises. The conclusion of such an argument may be true (consider *I* and *K*); the conclusion of such an argument may be false (consider

G and *M*). While we cannot know that the conclusion of a valid argument is true on the basis of knowing that the argument is valid, we do know that the conclusion of a valid argument would be true if all its premises were true. Consider *G*; if it were true that all athletes are professional golfers and that Arthur Ashe is an athlete, then it would be true that Arthur Ashe is a professional golfer.

If the premises of *G* were true, it would be a sound argument, a valid argument all of whose premises are true. The truth value of the sentences that constitute the premises and conclusion of an argument may differ from one time to another.[1] Thus the soundness of an argument may differ at different times. But the validity of an argument, the relation between its premises and its conclusion which we have expressed informally as guaranteeing the preservation of truth, cannot change. Of course, our ability to recognize or to demonstrate its validity may change. At the time this book is written, *E* is a sound argument. But if, for instance, Billie Jean King were no longer a professional tennis player, *E* would no longer be a sound argument, although its conclusion might remain true. But it would remain a valid argument, no less so if its conclusion were false.

An invalid argument does not guarantee the preservation of truth. The above discussion of *F* indicates that an argument can fail to guarantee that if its premises are true so also is its conclusion, even if its premises and conclusion are in fact true. But neither does an invalid argument guarantee that falsity in the premises will be preserved in the conclusion. In other words, an invalid argument may have one or more false premises and a true conclusion (consider *J* and *L*). Since a valid

---

[1] Here we are taking the premises and conclusions of arguments to be sentences. The material in chapter IV may lead the reader to prefer other ways of formulating this point.

argument does not guarantee the preservation of falsity (consider *I* and *K*), we can say that *no* argument guarantees that if one or more of its premises is false then so is its conclusion.

Of course an invalid argument with one or more false premises may have a false conclusion, as do arguments *H* and *N*. And an invalid argument, all of whose premises are true, may have a true conclusion (consider *F*) or a false conclusion (consider *O*). In short we may say that no invalid argument guarantees either that its conclusion is true or that it is false.

From the pair of arguments *I* and *J*, as well as *K* and *L*, we see that a sentence that is the conclusion of an invalid argument may be the conclusion of a valid argument also. If a sentence is the conclusion of an invalid argument, *that* argument does not guarantee its truth; it remains an open question whether there is a valid or a sound argument of which it is the conclusion.

Argument *O* has true premises and a false conclusion; so *O* is an obviously invalid argument. Among the invalid arguments above, *O* is the only one whose invalidity is obvious merely from the assertion of section 1 that an argument is valid just in case it is not possible for all its premises to be true while its conclusion is false. Argument *O* alone presents us with an actual instance of that possibility which is excluded for a valid argument. It is for this reason that no argument is paired with *O* as each other invalid argument is grouped with a valid argument. For there can be no valid argument whose premises are true and whose conclusion is false.

Of course not all invalid arguments display their invalidity in the truth values of their premises and conclusion; not all invalid arguments have premises that are in fact true and a conclusion that is in fact false. Argument *F*, for instance, has a true conclusion. To argue that it is invalid, we attempted to describe situations in which its premises would be true but its conclusion would be false. We did not have to argue that any such situation actually is the case. For an argument is invalid if it is possible that its premises are true while its conclusion is false. Argument *H*, for example, has a false premise; so its invalidity is not obvious from the truth values of its premises and conclusion alone. Again we attempt to describe a situation in which its premises would be true and argue that *H* is invalid by showing that in such a situation its conclusion might be false. Suppose it were true that all philosophers are Greeks and that Inge Broverman is a psychologist; it would still be possible that she is not Greek. Roughly speaking, even if the premises of *H* were true, they would offer no support, and certainly no guarantee, of the truth of the conclusion of *H*.

In arguing that *F* and *H* are invalid, we have relied on the informal account that an argument is valid if *but only if* it is not possible for its premises all to be true and its conclusion to be false. This technique of arguing that an argument is invalid is not singly adequate. Consider the following argument:

	(1)	All squares are polygons.	T	
P	(2)	All rectangles are polygons.	T	I
	(3)	All squares are rectangles.	T	

An attempt to describe a situation in which the conclusion of *P* would be false while its premises are true will fail. But it will fail not because the truth of the premises of *P* guarantees the truth of its conclusion. The truth of the conclusion of *P* is guaranteed by information which is no part of the argument. While this information from geometry supports the truth of the conclusion of *P*, it in no way strengthens the support which argument *P* provides for its conclusion. Indeed the conclusion of *P* could be the conclusion of a sound argument, but *P* is not that argument; for *P* is not a valid argument and so cannot be a sound argument. To argue that *P* is invalid, we might produce another argument which has the same *logical form* as *P* and has true premises and a false conclusion.

The concept of logical form is a complex one which has been the subject of considerable work among philosophers, implicitly at least since Leibniz and explicitly since Frege. Only a brief discussion of logical form can be undertaken in this book (see Chapter III, section 1), but the study of logic will provide the student with tools enabling increasingly detailed analysis of form. Argument *O* has the same logical form as *P*. This fact, for which the reader will find evidence in Chapter III, section 1, conjoined with the fact that *O* has true premises and a false conclusion, provides an excellent argument that *P* is invalid. For an argument is valid just in case no argument with the same form has all true premises and a false conclusion.[2]

We have said that the goal of logic is to preserve truth and that, pursuant to this goal, the most basic mark of quality in an argument is validity. The reader may wonder why, then, in this section we have discussed techniques which may be used to provide evidence that an argument is invalid but not that an argument is valid. Recalling the informal accounts of validity that have been given will provide a partial answer. An argument is valid just in case it is *not possible* that its premises are all true while its conclusion is false. To capitalize

---

[2] We have regarded an argument as a group of sentences, one of which is identified as its conclusion and the remainder of which are regarded as premises. If instead we were to consider an argument as all such groups of sentences having the same form, these two informal accounts of validity converge.

on this account in an effort to establish that an argument is valid, we would have to survey *all* possibilities to determine that none of them provides a situation in which all the premises of the argument are true while its conclusion is false. Such a survey itself is not possible in any finite period of time! But a single situation in which the premises are all true and the conclusion false obviously is sufficient to show that such a situation is possible and that the argument cannot be valid. An argument is valid if and only if *no* argument with the same form has all true premises and a false conclusion. Analogously, to capitalize on this account in order to establish that an argument is valid, we would have to survey all arguments (actual and possible?) which have the same form. Such a survey is equally beyond what is possible for finite humans.

Because of these and other difficulties in establishing the validity of an argument considered in isolation rather than as exemplifying the logical form on which its validity or invalidity depends, the tools of formal logic are extremely valuable. Within the study of logic, special symbolism or notation is developed which enables us to study the forms of arguments and to isolate many of the formal components of sentences, on which components the validity of arguments depends. Precise rules can be stated in terms of the forms of sentences, and the deductive methods available enable us to evaluate arguments to the extent that their form can be expressed in the symbolic notation available to us. In addition to the informal accounts of validity already mentioned, we can say that an argument is valid if and only if its conclusion is a logical consequence of its premises. The methods of formal logic put us in a position better to understand the content of this and other informal accounts of validity. Presentation and discussion of these methods are beyond the scope of this book. However, we shall attempt, in the remaining section of this chapter and in Chapter II, to introduce the reader to some of the most basic formal components of arguments.

Many philosophers claim that the existing tools of formal logic are inadequate to express, and therefore to evaluate, the forms of many interesting arguments. If so, this claim provides an incentive for further developments in logic, but it is no criticism of the value of the existing tools of logic in evaluating the arguments whose logical forms these tools enable us to reveal.

Not all arguments are of the three-line form we have been considering. And not all arguments which are of that form appear at first glance to be so. For example:

Q
    (1) Caesar is emperor.

    (2) (Therefore) Someone is emperor.

is a simple argument that is sound but has a different form. And:

R
    (1) Jones is a man.

    (2) (Therefore) Jones is mortal.

is an argument that is valid only on the strength of the suppressed (or unexpressed) premise that all men are mortal. Such an argument is clearly valid, and of the familiar three-line form, *if* we add the missing premise. If we do not, we can consider the argument as incomplete rather than invalid.

And of course not all arguments are either as simple in their structure or as obvious in their validity or invalidity as those we have considered. In fact few arguments are, whether they are found in the writings of a famous philosopher, in one's own writings, in editorials, in political debates, or in advertisements. We have attempted to choose as examples arguments about which the reader will have accurate intuitions concerning their validity or invalidity. Since intuitions are not infallible guides to validity, especially as arguments increase in their complexity, we have sought to strengthen these intuitions and to provide the reader with ways to support his or her evaluation of arguments. In the discussion of validity and its relations to the actual and possible truth value of premises and conclusions, we hope the reader will find an increased understanding of the concept of validity which will sharpen intuitions involved in assessing arguments. And we have attempted to suggest ways of structuring these intuitions so that they may be extended and applied constructively to less explicitly structured and more complex arguments.

3. Propositional Logic

Let us now consider some of the basic features of symbolic logic, a discipline that, in addition to performing other functions, provides techniques for determining both the validity of some kinds of argument and the consistency of sets of sentences.

Assume that each sentence we are considering has exactly one of two possible truth values at any given time. Above, we used 'T' or 'F' to indicate the truth or falsity of sentences in arguments $E-P$. Let us now adopt this notation officially and indicate that a sentence is true by using 'T' and that a sentence is false by using 'F'.

Consider the sentences 'New York is the most populous city in the U.S.A.' and 'San Francisco is in Illinois'. We shall let the capital letters 'P', 'Q', and 'R' (with or without subscripts)[3] serve as abbreviations for sentences, allowing each letter to abbreviate *only one* sentence in any given context. Here, let 'P' abbreviate the sentence 'New York is the most populous city in the U.S.A.' and let 'Q' abbreviate 'San Francisco is in Illinois'. The sentence abbreviated by 'P' is true; so it has the truth value T. The sentence abbreviated by 'Q' is false and so has the truth value F. Now the sentence 'New York is not the most populous city in the U.S.A.' is not true. We can rewrite this sentence as 'It is not the case that New York is the most populous city in the U.S.A.' By taking advantage of our abbreviation, we obtain 'It is not the case that P'. Creating new sentences by prefixing the phrase 'it is not the case that' to a sentence produces a *negation* of the original sentence, which follows the phrase 'it is not the case that'. By letting a short wavy stroke '∼' represent this phrase, we may shorten our abbreviation of 'It is not the case that P' to '∼P', and we may abbreviate 'San Francisco is not in Illinois" as '∼Q'.[4]

Because we wish to talk about characteristics that all sentences having the same logical form have in common, we

---

[3] We provide for the use of subscripts here and elsewhere to ensure that an adequate supply of *different* symbols is available. 'P' and 'P_0' are sentence letters; each may be used to abbreviate a sentence. They are different one from another and each from either 'Q' or 'Q_3'.

[4] In many cases, such substitutions as 'fails to be' for 'is not' and either 'it is not true that' or 'it is false that' for 'it is not the case that' will produce sentences which are subject to this pattern of abbreviation.

shall use Greek letters in order to talk about the logical form of sentences.[5] Thus, if Φ is any sentence, then the result of writing ' ∼ ' followed by Φ is the negation of Φ. Where Φ is any sentence, we exhibit the form of the negation of Φ by:

$$\sim \Phi.$$

Obviously if Φ is a true sentence, then ∼ Φ is a false sentence;[6] and if Φ is false, then ∼ Φ is true. We can illustrate these features of negation with the following diagram, called a truth table:

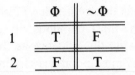

	Φ	∼ Φ
1	T	F
2	F	T

This table is the truth table for negation. Rows 1 and 2 represent the only possibilities for the truth value of any sentence Φ; either Φ is true or it is false, and it is not both. The second column shows that when Φ is true (first column, row 1), then ∼ Φ is false and that when Φ is false (first column, row 2), then ∼ Φ is true. On the basis of this truth table, we

---

[5] We use each of the Greek letters 'Φ' and 'Ψ' to stand for any sentence whatsoever. In particular we will use them as if they were part of English in English sentences in which we talk about sentences formed by using sentence letters and connectives. (The letter 'Φ' is sometimes pronounced 'fee', sometimes 'fie'; and 'Ψ' is sometimes pronounced 'psee', sometimes 'psigh'.) This practice enables us to talk about sentences without using the name of any particular sentence. While this practice may appear complicating, the reader will see in Chapter VIII, section 3, why we cannot use, for instance, either 'P' or "P" to talk about an arbitrary sentence, just any sentence whatsoever.

[6] In predicating 'is a false sentence' of ' ∼ Φ' we are not being strictly correct, as the reader who further pursues the study of logic will discover. It would, however, be unnecessarily complicated for our purposes to be strictly correct in our usage of the Greek letters in combination with sentential connectives, such as ' ∼ ' and parentheses. We believe that our usage will not be confusing.

can see that the negation of the false sentence 'San Francisco is in Illinois' is true and that the negation of this negation, that is, '$\sim\sim Q$', is false. In general, (a) Φ is true and $\sim\Phi$ is false just in case $\sim\sim\Phi$ is true; and (b) Φ is false and $\sim\Phi$ is true just in case $\sim\sim\Phi$ is false.

Now let us consider the word 'and'. By placing 'and' between any two declarative sentences, Φ and Ψ, we can form a third sentence, the *conjunction* of Φ and Ψ. Letting '&' represent 'and',[7] we form the conjunction of Φ and Ψ by writing '(', followed by Φ, followed by '&', followed by Ψ, followed by ')'. That is, we exhibit the form of the conjunction of Φ and Ψ by:

$$(\Phi \ \& \ \Psi).$$

What do we know about the truth value of conjunctions? Consider the sentence 'It is raining and it is Tuesday'. This sentence is true only in case it *is* raining *and* it *is* Tuesday. Otherwise it is false. In general $(\Phi \ \& \ \Psi)$ is true if Φ is true and Ψ is true; otherwise $(\Phi \ \& \ \Psi)$ is false. We can illustrate the truth conditions for conjunctions with a truth table:

Φ	Ψ	$(\Phi \ \& \ \Psi)$
T	T	T
T	F	F
F	T	F
F	F	F

---

[7] The symbol '&' is also used to indicate a feature common to such compound and complex sentences as:

Both Φ and Ψ	Although Φ, Ψ
Φ, and Ψ	Ψ although Φ
Φ; Ψ	Even though Φ, Ψ
Φ, but Ψ	Ψ even though Φ

Here there are four rows, one for each possible combination of truth values for any two sentences Φ and Ψ.

We call '&' a sentential connective, since with it we are able to connect sentences and thereby form new sentences. Similarly, although we do not use ' ~ ' to *connect* sentences, we call ' ~ ' a connective. The symbol '&' is a two-place connective—we use it between two sentences; ' ~ ' is a one-place connective—we use it with one sentence. But of course that one sentence which is negated may itself be quite complex. When Ψ is a sentence, ~Ψ is a sentence; so when Φ and Ψ are sentences, (Φ & ~ Ψ) is a sentence, and so also is ~(Φ & ~Ψ) a sentence. Notice that ~(Φ & ~ Ψ), which has the form of the negation of a conjunction, is different from (~Φ & ~Ψ), which has the form of a conjunction of two negations.

Now we can form new sentences in many ways. Starting with any sentences Φ and Ψ, we can, for example, produce sentences of any of the following forms:

$$\sim \Phi$$
$$(\Psi \, \& \sim \Phi)$$
$$(\sim \Phi \, \& \sim \Psi)$$
$$\sim (\Phi \, \& \sim \Psi).$$

It is a simple matter to construct truth tables for any of these; for given the truth values of any two sentences Φ and Ψ, we can compute the truth value of any compound produced from these sentences using our two sentential connectives. Consider: ~(Φ & ~Ψ).

Φ	Ψ	~Ψ	(Φ & ~Ψ)	~(Φ & ~Ψ)
T	T	F	F	T
T	F	T	T	F
F	T	F	F	T
F	F	T	F	T

Given the truth value of any sentence Ψ, we can use the truth table for negation to compute the truth value of ∼Ψ. And given any combination of truth values for Φ and ∼Ψ, we can use the truth table for conjunction to compute the truth value (Φ & ∼Ψ). Finally, using the truth value for (Φ & ∼Ψ), we can use the truth table for negation once again to compute the truth value of ∼(Φ & ∼Ψ). This table shows us the truth conditions for the negation of the conjunction of any sentence and the negation of any sentence. It shows us that any sentence of the form ∼(Φ & ∼Ψ) will be false if Φ is true and Ψ is false; otherwise it will be true. For example, if and only if it is raining but it is not Tuesday, the sentence 'It is not the case both that it is raining and that it is not Tuesday' is false.

We may now consider three more sentential connectives. We shall use '∨' to represent 'or'. This connective is the disjunction sign. The logical form of a *disjunction* is:

$$(\Phi \vee \Psi).$$

The truth table for disjunction is:

Φ	Ψ	(Φ ∨ Ψ)
T	T	T
T	F	T
F	T	T
F	F	F

That is, if Φ and Ψ are both false sentences, then (Φ ∨ Ψ) is false; otherwise (Φ ∨ Ψ) is true. Disjunction as characterized by this truth table may be said to be inclusive, in that the disjunction is true if both of the disjuncts are true. For example, 'Either it will rain today or it will snow today' is true if it will both rain and snow today. Sometimes we may

intend to rule out its being possible that both disjuncts of
a true disjunction are true; that is, we may intend an exclusive
disjunction. For example, the father who says 'We will go on
a picnic or we will go to a movie' may intend to rule out
doing both. Using our present connectives, we could make
such an intention explicit by using a sentence having the form:

$$[(\Phi \vee \Psi) \mathbin{\&} \sim(\Phi \mathbin{\&} \Psi)].$$

In fact, the father in our example might well use a sentence
of just this form to make his intention explicit; thus: 'Either
we will go on a picnic or we will go to a movie, but not
both'.

The next connective we introduce is an arrow: '→'. It will
be useful, at least at first, to think of sentences having the form:

$$(\Phi \rightarrow \Psi)$$

as abbreviations for sentences having the form:

$$(\sim\Phi \vee \Psi).$$

The truth table for sentences of either form is the same:

Φ	Ψ	$\sim\Phi$	$(\sim\Phi \vee \Psi)$	$(\Phi \rightarrow \Psi)$
T	T	F	T	T
T	F	F	F	F
F	T	T	T	T
F	F	T	T	T

Further, by comparing this truth table with that given above for sentences of the form:

$$\sim(\Phi \mathrel{\&} \sim\Psi)$$

we see that the truth tables do not distinguish between them. Sentences which are not distinguished from one another by their final truth table analysis are said to be truth-functionally equivalent. They may also be said to be logically equivalent. Logical equivalence is the broader notion; all truth-functionally equivalent sentences are logically equivalent sentences. But many sentences are logically equivalent which are not truth-functionally equivalent; the logical equivalence of such sentences depends on form which cannot be revealed by truth-functional analysis alone. Sentences which are truth-functionally equivalent are sometimes also said to have the same truth conditions.

Our primary reason for introducing this new connective is that sentences of the form:

$$(\Phi \rightarrow \Psi)$$

reflect at least one important feature of English sentences of the form:

If Φ, then Ψ.

Such sentences—for example, 'If it is raining, then I will stay home'—are called conditional sentences. The sentence following 'If' (in this case, 'it is raining') is called the *antecedent*, while the sentence following 'then' (in this case,

'I will stay home') is called the *consequent*. The feature of such sentences reflected by sentences of the form:

$$(\Phi \rightarrow \Psi)$$

is that it is a basic part of the meaning of a conditional sentence that, if the antecedent is true and the consequent is false, then the entire conditional sentence is false. Thus, using the example above, if it is in fact raining, but I do not stay home, we would say that the statement 'If it is raining, then I will stay home' is false. We shall call any sentence of the form:

$$(\Phi \rightarrow \Psi)$$

a conditional sentence and use ' $\rightarrow$ ' as a representation of the phrase 'if ... , then ...' as it occurs in sentences of the form:

$$\text{If } \Phi, \text{ then } \Psi.^8$$

---

[8] There are a great many ways to form English conditionals. Following is a partial list:

If Φ, then Ψ	Given that Φ, Ψ
Φ only if Ψ	Only if Ψ, Φ
Ψ if Φ	Ψ provided that Φ
Ψ in case Φ	Ψ assuming that Φ
Ψ on the condition that Φ	

All these conditionals share the feature of being false when Φ is true but Ψ is false.

Note also that the following sentences share with $(\Phi \vee \Psi)$ the feature that they are false if Φ is false and Ψ is false:

Ψ unless Φ
Unless Φ, Ψ
If $\sim\Phi$, then Ψ

We do *not* take ' → ' to be an abbreviation of 'implies'. We take implication to be a relation that holds between a sentence Φ and a sentence Ψ if Ψ is a logical consequence of Φ. Two specific examples will be helpful:

> (1) If the horse's leg is broken, then the horse will be shot.
> (2) 'The horse's leg is broken' implies 'The horse will be shot'.

Note that because (2) expresses a relationship (implication) between sentences, it contains two sentence names which have been formed by putting the sentences they name within single quote marks. (See Chapter VIII, section 3.) On the other hand (1), which does *not* express a relationship between sentences, does not contain any names of sentences. The first sentence may very well be true, but the second is not. For 'The horse will be shot' is not a logical consequence of 'The horse's leg is broken'.

Notice that it would be incorrect to interpret the truth table for conditionals as a truth table for implication even if we disregard the fact that 'implies' requires names of sentences, not sentences, on each side of it in order to produce a sentence. The difficulty is this: We would have to say that every sentence implies each true sentence and that each false sentence implies every sentence. (Consider lines 1, 3, and 4 of the truth table.) Consequently we shall treat 'implies' as expressing a relation between sentences, not as a phrase of connection enabling us to produce more complex sentences from simpler sentences— in other words, not as a sentential connective. (See the discussion of 'imply', 'infer', and 'entail', in Chapter III, section 1.)

Someone may well feel that it is also incorrect to suppose that it is true that if Plato was a Greek, then General Motors produces Chevrolets. And surely the truth table for conditionals does commit us to this. (Consider line 1.) But we must be very cautious here. It is very unusual to find conditional sentences the antecedent and the consequent of which are about totally unrelated things. But once we recognize that such conditionals are possible, we find that it would be as peculiar to say that 'If Plato was a Greek, then General Motors produces Chevrolets' is false as it is to say that it is true. The oddity, then, arises not from considering such sentences to be true; rather, it arises from considering them at all.

An even more serious conflict with our initial intuitions arises when we consider the following conditional sentences and refer to lines 3 and 4 of the truth table for conditionals:

(i) If Dionysius was born in 335 B.C., then Dionysius was born before 335 B.C.

(ii) If Dionysius was born in 335 B.C., then Dionysius was not born in 1950.

(iii) If Dionysius was born in 335 B.C., then Dionysius was born before 334 B.C.

(iv) If Dionysius was born in 335 B.C., then Dionysius was born in 330 B.C.

Now assuming that Dionysius was born in 330 B.C., sentences (i)–(iv) all have false antecedents, and sentences (ii) and (iv) have true consequents. According to the truth table for conditionals, all four sentences are true since all have false antecedents. Yet most speakers of English would initially take only (ii) and (iii) to be true. We can represent this discrepancy as follows:

According to the truth table for '→', sentences (i)–(iv) would be true as follows:

According to our intuitive understanding of conditionals:

   (i) F → F : T   (i) is F

   (ii) F → T : T   (ii) is T

   (iii) F → F : T   (iii) is T

   (iv) F → T : T   (iv) is F

This shows that the truth table for sentences of the form:

$$(\Phi \rightarrow \Psi)$$

does not adequately reflect *all* our intuitions about conditional sentences in English. Moreover, it shows that no connective whose meaning could be given by means of a truth table could possibly capture *all* our initial intuitions about conditionals. For (i) and (iii) would both be represented by the same row of any truth table, as would (ii) and (iv). Yet according to our initial intuitions, (i) and (iii) differ in truth value, as do (ii) and (iv). We shall nonetheless use the truth table given for conditionals, bearing in mind these difficulties and remembering that sometimes—after thorough reflection—we come to give up our initial intuitions.

We face similar difficulties if we try to capture our intuitions about sentences formed in English by using 'unless' with a connective whose meaning is given by means of a truth table. We choose to treat a sentence

$$\Psi \text{ unless } \Phi$$

as we treat

If it is not the case that Φ, then Ψ.

However, many logic texts recommend symbolization of 'unless' by '∨'. It is easy to demonstrate that truth-value analysis will reveal no difference between these two treatments. For the final truth tables for the resulting conditional and disjunction are the same.[9] Let us consider some other examples. Suppose we know that Anne is a Capricorn, but we do not know whether or not Anne will become a lawyer. What are our intuitions about the following sentences?

(i) Anne will not become a lawyer unless Anne is a Capricorn.
(ii) Either Anne will not become a lawyer or Anne is a Capricorn.
(iii) Anne will not become a lawyer if Anne is not a Capricorn.

Although we might find (ii) a peculiar sentence, we would probably be willing to acknowledge that it is true because it is true that Anne is a Capricorn. On the other hand we would be strongly inclined to assess both (i) and (iii) as false. Notice that even if we would not be willing to assess (i) and (iii) as false, we would certainly *not* be willing to acknowledge either as true merely on the basis of the truth of the sentence 'Anne is a Capricorn'. Sentence (ii) would be symbolized as a disjunction; (iii) would be symbolized as a conditional; (i) might be symbolized either as a disjunction or as a conditional. And each of the resulting symbolic sentences will have the truth value true when the sentence 'Anne is a Capricorn' is true.

Finally we introduce the connective '↔' as a representation of 'if and only if'.[10] Sentences having the logical form:

$$(\Phi \leftrightarrow \Psi)$$

[9] See exercise 8.
[10] Many occurrences of 'if and only if' can be replaced, without significantly altering the information conveyed, by 'if but only if', 'exactly on the condition that', or 'just in case'.

are called *biconditionals*. The reason for this characterization becomes obvious when we note that the truth conditions for biconditionals are the same as those for sentences of the form:

$$[(\Psi \to \Phi) \,\&\, (\Phi \to \Psi)]$$

Φ	Ψ	$(\Phi \leftrightarrow \Psi)$	$(\Psi \to \Phi)$	$(\Phi \to \Psi)$	$[(\Psi \to \Phi) \,\&\, (\Phi \to \Psi)]$
T	T	T	T	T	T
T	F	F	T	F	F
F	T	F	F	T	F
F	F	T	T	T	T

To review, we have five connectives:[11]

not	$\sim$
and	$\&$
or	$\vee$
if . . . , then	$\to$
if and only if	$\leftrightarrow$

[11] The following table indicates some alternative symbolizations in common use. Instead of:

$\sim P$:	$\overline{P}, \vdash P,$	$-P,$		or NP
$(P \,\&\, Q)$:	$(P \cdot Q),$	$(P \wedge Q),$	$(PQ),$	or KPQ
$(P \vee Q)$:				or APQ
$(P \to Q)$:	$(P \supset Q)$			or CPQ
$(P \leftrightarrow Q)$:	$(P \equiv Q)$			or EPQ

The last column is Polish notation, which eliminates the need for parentheses by a conventional ordering of symbols. We could also have a parenthesis-free notation by using our symbols as letters for connectives are used in Polish notation: $\sim P$, $\&PQ$, $\vee PQ$, $\to PQ$, $\leftrightarrow PQ$. Then, for instance, '$(P \vee \sim R)$' would be written as '$\vee P \sim R$'.

Now consider the symbolization of some simple sentences:[12]

If you come, I won't drive.

   P: You come.
   Q: I will drive.

$$(P \rightarrow \sim Q)$$

Prices will drop if but only if either taxes are lowered or workers will not strike.

   P: Prices will drop.
   Q: Taxes are lowered.
   R: Workers will strike.

$$[P \leftrightarrow (Q \vee \sim R)]$$

It is raining and it is not raining.

   P: It is raining.

$$(P \mathrel{\&} \sim P)$$

It is raining or it is not raining.

$$(P \vee \sim P)$$

Compare the truth tables for sentences having the same forms as these last two sentences:

Φ	$\sim\Phi$	$(\Phi \mathrel{\&} \sim\Phi)$	$(\Phi \vee \sim\Phi)$
T	F	F	T
F	T	F	T

[12] Expressions like "P: You come" will be used in place of the more cumbersome: "Let 'P' abbreviate the sentence 'You come'."

Sentences having the form:

$$(\Phi \;\&\; \sim\Phi)$$

are said to be contradictions. And sentences having the form:

$$(\Phi \vee \sim\Phi)$$

are said to be tautologies. More generally, any sentence whose *form* is such that a truth table for sentences of that form reveals that the sentence is always false is said to be a contradiction and is *logically* false. And any sentence whose *form* is such that a truth table for sentences of that form reveals that the sentence is always true is said to be a tautology and is *logically* true. Of course, not all false sentences are contradictions, nor are all true sentences tautologies.

The concepts of a logically false sentence and a logically true sentence are broader than the concepts of a contradiction and a tautology as defined here. That is, all contradictions are logically false, but not all logically false sentences are contradictions. Similarly, all tautologies are logically true, but not all logically true sentences are tautologies. For example, 'Some yellow house is not a house' is logically false; but no truth table will reveal that it is always false. And 'All lawyers are lawyers' is logically true, but no truth table will reveal that it is always true.

We may now introduce the notion of *consistency*. We say that a set of sentences is consistent if it is possible that all the sentences in the set are true. Thus the set:

(1) $(P \rightarrow Q)$
(2) $(R \rightarrow \sim Q)$
(3) P
(4) R

is an *inconsistent* set. Consider the truth table for conditionals and the one for conjunctions. According to the truth table for conditionals, if (1) and (3) are true, then it is true that Q; and if (2) and (4) are true, then it is true that $\sim$Q. But according to the truth table for conjunction, if it is true that Q and it is true that $\sim$Q, then it is true that (Q & $\sim$Q). But we have seen that it is not possible for any sentence having the form:

$$(\Phi \ \& \ \sim\Phi)$$

to be true. So it is not possible for all the sentences in this set to be true; therefore the set that consists of sentences (1), (2), (3), and (4) is inconsistent.

Finally, consider again the sentence 'All lawyers are lawyers'. This sentence, although logically true, has no sentential connectives. Thus the only truth table possible for this sentence is the one for sentences having the form Φ. And this truth table is:

$$\frac{\Phi}{\begin{array}{c} \text{T} \\ \hline \text{F} \end{array}}$$

Whether or not a sentence is logically true depends on its logical form. Such a table, obviously, does not reveal the logical form in virtue of which 'All lawyers are lawyers' is logically true. To exhibit the logical form of such sentences, we need a much more powerful set of techniques. A small part of these techniques will be considered in the next chapter.

Exercises

1. What does it mean to say of an argument that it is sound? valid? Illustrate the difference with examples.

2. Present the best argument you can that argument N (section 2) is invalid.

*3. Each argument can be represented by a profile that indicates the truth value of each line in the argument and also the validity and soundness of the argument. For example, in:

Premise$_1$	All people breathe.
Premise$_2$	Jones is a person.
Conclusion	Jones breathes.

the premises and conclusion are true, and the argument is valid and sound. We can therefore write its profile as:

T
T
T
V
S.

On the other hand:

Premise$_3$	All men are mortal.
Premise$_4$	Fish live in trees.
Conclusion	Birds fly.

has a profile of:

T
F
T
I
U.

Whereas a profile can be written for each argument, it is not the case that an argument can be found to correspond to each profile. For instance, no argument can have:

T
T
F
V
S

as its profile, because

T
T
F

is incompatible with V (which means the conclusion cannot be false if the premises are true).

Write down six possible profiles for arguments with two premises, and for each one either give an example of an argument that clearly has that profile or else explain in detail exactly why no such argument can be found.

4. If the conclusion of a valid argument is a logically false sentence, what can we say about the truth values of the premises of that argument?

*5. Is [~(P & ~Q) ↔ (P → Q)] a tautology, a contradiction, or neither? Justify your answer by constructing a truth table.

6. Is [~(P & Q) ↔ (~P ∨ Q)] a tautology, a contradiction, or neither? Justify your answer by constructing a truth table.

7. Give an example to show that not only tautologies are true.

8. Is (~P → Q) equivalent to (Q ∨ P)? Prove with truth tables that your answer is correct.

*9. A. Symbolize the following sentences using 'P' for 'The sun shines' and 'Q' for 'I'll be at the beach':
    (a) If the sun shines, I'll be at the beach.
    (b) I'll be at the beach unless the sun doesn't shine.
    (c) Either the sun doesn't shine or I'll be at the beach.
    (d) It is not the case that both the sun shines and I'll not be at the beach.
  B. From the truth tables that give the truth conditions for the symbolizations of sentences (a) through (d), what can we say about the logical relations (consistency, logical equivalence, and implication) among these four sentences?

*10. Symbolize the following sentences, indicating the abbreviations you are using for each sentence:
    (a) You read with care or you learn little.
    (b) If there is smoke, there is fire.

(c) Helen will camp if the moon is full, but otherwise not.

(d) All scholars ruminate.

(e) Johnny may have cake or ice cream, but not both.

11. Express the exclusive sense of disjunction in terms of ' $\sim$ ', '&', and ' $\vee$ ', and show by a truth table that your expression is correct.

II

Predicate Calculus and Sets

1. Predicate Calculus

The concepts and symbols introduced thus far do not allow us to exhibit the logical form of such sentences as 'All brothers are male siblings'. The general claim exemplified by this sentence is that all things having a certain property (that of being a brother, in this case) also have another property (that of being a male sibling). To symbolize such a sentence merely as 'P' leaves the details of its internal structure inexplicit.

The symbols introduced in Chapter I allow us to represent some of the formal structure between sentences, but these symbols are inadequate to enable us to reveal structure within a sentence that is not sententially complex. Yet it is often this internal structure that determines the truth conditions of a sentence and thus its role in an argument.

In what follows, the concepts and techniques for exhibiting the logical form of simple sentences will be developed, so that we will have a more powerful method for the analysis of sentences and so for understanding their truth conditions.

As an example of an obviously valid argument, consider:

> All Athenians are wise.
> Callias is an Athenian.
> (Therefore) Callias is wise.

As a first step in symbolizing this argument, we abbreviate the name 'Callias' with 'c'. We shall use lower-case letters (with or without subscripts, but excluding 'x', 'y', and 'z') to denote particular individuals; such terms are called *individual constants*. We use constants to abbreviate not only proper names such as 'Callias' but also definite descriptions such as 'the wisest scholar in Athens'. We may, for example, let the constant 'd' abbreviate the phrase 'the wisest scholar in Athens'.

The sentence 'Callias is wise' consists of a subject ('Callias') and a *predicate* ('is wise'). We shall abbreviate predicates by capital letters (with or without subscripts).[1] In this case, let us replace 'is wise' by the *predicate symbol* 'W'. We shall adopt the convention of writing the constant abbreviating the subject of predication immediately after the predicate symbol, so that 'Callias is wise' will be symbolized by 'Wc'.

It is often true that a particular sentence can be symbolized in several different ways. As an example, consider:

> Callias is wise and Callias is an Athenian.

This sentence can be symbolized in at least two ways:

---

[1] We except 'P', 'Q', and 'R', which are reserved for abbreviation of sentences. See the discussion of propositional logic in section 3 of Chapter I.

(a) On the basis of the scheme of abbreviation:

W: is wise
A: is an Athenian
c: Callias

(Wc & Ac).

(b) On the basis of the scheme of abbreviation:

B: is wise and is an Athenian
c: Callias

Bc.

Which of these symbolizations of the original sentence is chosen will depend on the purposes for which the English sentence is being symbolized. However, the symbolization ('Wc and Ac') reveals more of the structure of the example sentence than does 'Bc' and, for this reason, is the more interesting for most of the purposes for which sentences are usually symbolized.

The predicate 'is wise' is a *one-place* predicate because the result of writing the predicate symbol which abbreviates it followed by one individual constant is a sentence. Some predicates are two-place—for example, 'loves'. 'John loves Mary' may be symbolized by 'Ljm' on the basis of the scheme of abbreviation:

$$L(1)(2): (1) \text{ loves } (2).^2$$
$$j: \text{John}$$
$$m: \text{Mary}$$

---

[2] Notice that 'John loves Mary' and 'Mary loves John' are different sentences, although each is composed of the same predicate and names. In general, the order of individual constants following a two-or-more-place predicate symbol must be indicated in the scheme of abbreviation. We shall also indicate the subject position for one-place predicates.

And, of course, there are higher-place predicates, such as 'lies between' in the sentence 'Point a lies between points b and f', symbolized by 'Babf' on the basis of:

$$B \ (1)(2)(3): \ (1) \text{ lies between } (2) \text{ and } (3)$$
$$\text{a: point } a$$
$$\text{b: point } b$$
$$\text{f: point } f.$$

Note that verbs are not the only words that can be symbolized by predicate symbols (as the word 'predicate' may lead one to expect). Adjectival, adverbial, and prepositional phrases are often represented in the language of the predicate calculus by predicate symbols. While this treatment is not free of difficulties, it remains widely accepted. Consider, for instance, the sentence 'Callias talks in the Academy with Plato'. We can treat everything after the word 'Callias' as a predicate and symbolize the sentence by 'Tc' on the basis of the scheme of abbreviation:

$$T \ (1): \ (1) \text{ talks in the Academy with Plato}$$
$$\text{c: Callias.}$$

On the other hand, we may treat the predicate as a two-place predicate, symbolizing the sentence by 'T_1cp' on the basis of the scheme:

$$T_1(1) \ (2): \ (1) \text{ talks in the Academy with } (2)$$
$$\text{c: Callias}$$
$$\text{p: Plato.}$$

In general, a one-place predicate may be constructed from a two-place predicate by filling one of the places in the latter with a name or definite description (as 'Plato' was added to the predicate 'talks in the Academy with' to form the one-place predicate 'talks in the Academy with Plato').

Consider the symbolization of the following sentences:

Callias is wise.	Wc
Socrates is wise.	Ws
Aristophanes is wise.	Wa

The form or pattern common to these expressions may be indicated by introducing *individual variables* such as 'x' in the expression 'Wx'. (We shall use 'x', 'y', and 'z', with or without subscripts, for variables.) Such variables do not denote any particular individual. Rather, they may take as their values any entity in the universe of discourse. In some respects, a variable may be thought of as corresponding to a pronoun in ordinary language. Since Callias is wise, we may truly say:

(1) There exists someone, such that he is wise.

In symbolizing (1), we must make use of a variable, since the 'he' in (1) does not refer to any specified person, only to *someone*. Therefore, we begin the symbolization of (1) as follows:

(1a) There exists an x such that x is wise.[3]
(1b) There exists an x such that Wx.

---

[3] To capture the use of some*one* for persons, it would be better to write 'There exists an x such that x is a person and x is wise.' But for the purposes of this discussion, we follow the common practice of not distinguishing 'some*one*' from 'some*thing*' or 'every*one*' from 'every*thing*'.

Finally, we introduce the *quantifier* '($\exists$x)' to stand for 'There exists an x such that':

(1c) ($\exists$x) Wx.

(Note the use of parentheses to set off the quantifier from the rest of the sentence.)

Of course, it makes no difference which variable we use; (1) could just as well have been translated by '($\exists$y) Wy'.

The quantifier '($\exists$x)' is also read as 'for some x' or 'there is at least one x such that'.

Next, consider the sentence:

(2)   Everything in the universe is green. That is,
(2a) Each thing x is such that it is green. Or,
(2b) Each thing x is such that x is green.

We introduce the quantifier '(x)' for 'Each thing x is such that'. Then on the basis of the scheme of abbreviation:

G (*1*): (*1*) is green.

Sentence (2) may be symbolized by:

(2c) (x) Gx.

(Here again 'y' could have been used in place of 'x'.)

The quantifier ($\exists$x) is called the *existential* quantifier; (x) is called the *universal* quantifier.[4]

---

[4] Some other symbols used for quantifiers are:

Instead of:

($\exists$x)	(Ex), Vx
(x)	($\forall$x), Λx

Following are some examples of the translation of English sentences into the symbolic logic notation just introduced. The following scheme of abbreviation is adopted for these examples:

> A(*1*): (*1*) is an Athenian
> C(*1*): (*1*) is a Cretan
> W(*1*): (*1*) is wise
> S(*1*)(*2*): (*1*) is smarter than (*2*).

(1) All Athenians are wise.

That is:

(1a) Each thing is such that if it is an Athenian, then it is wise.
(1b) (x) (Ax → Wx).

One may be tempted to translate (1) by:

(1c) (x) (Ax & Wx).

But (1c) is clearly incorrect, for it says that each thing is such that it is an Athenian *and* it is wise. So its closest English translation is 'All things are Athenians and are wise', which has not at all the same meaning or truth conditions as (1).

(2)   Some Athenians are wise.
(2a) There is at least one thing such that it is an Athenian and it is wise.
(2b) (∃x) (Ax & Wx).

In the case of this second example, it would be *incorrect* to write:

(2c) (∃x) (Ax → Wx),

because (2) is true only if there exists at least one wise Athenian, whereas (2c) may be true even if there are *no* wise Athenians. For (2c) says that something is such that if it is an Athenian, then it is wise. So (2c) is true if there is one thing of which the conditional is true. And the conditional is true of things that are not Athenians. This can be seen by referring back to the truth table for conditionals and noting that expressions having the form:

$$(\Phi \rightarrow \Psi)$$

have the same truth table as expressions having the form:

$$(\sim \Phi \vee \Psi).$$

Thus, '(Ax → Wx)' and '(∼Ax ∨ Wx)' are equivalent; therefore we may replace (2c) by:

(2d) (∃x) (∼Ax ∨ Wx).

But (2d) is true when there exists something that either is *not* an Athenian or *is* wise, so (2d) is true so long as there is at least one thing that is not an Athenian. Thus (2d), which is equivalent to (2c), can be true even when there are *no* wise Athenians, and it is clear that (2c) is not the correct translation of (2).

A third example illustrates the use of more than one quantifier:

(3) Every Athenian is smarter than each Cretan.

(3a) Each thing x and each thing y are such that if x is an Athenian and y is a Cretan, then x is smarter than y.

(3b) (x) (y) ((Ax & Cy) → Sxy).

Some sentences may be symbolized in more than one way. Consider for instance:

(4) Some Athenians are not wise.

First consider it as a denial of (1):

(4a) It is not the case that all Athenians are wise.

(4b) ~(x) (Ax → Wx).

Or we can paraphrase (4) by:

(4c) There is at least one thing such that it is an Athenian and it is not wise.

(4d) (∃x) (Ax & ~Wx).

Actually, it can be shown that (4b) and (4d) are equivalent in the sense that each follows logically from the other.

Finally, we shall symbolize the argument with which this section began:

(I) All Athenians are wise.
     Callias is an Athenian.
     (Therefore) Callias is wise.

(Ia) (x) (Ax → Wx)
     Ac
     ∴ Wc.

The argument is clearly valid, because if it is true of all individuals that, if they are Athenians, then they are wise, then it is certainly true of any particular individual, say c, that if c is an Athenian, c is wise. The second premise tells us that c is indeed an Athenian. Therefore, c is wise.

But not all arguments are so transparent, and it is necessary to specify exactly and in detail what sort of inferences can be made legitimately. This is done by means of a set of rules usually called *rules of inference*. One common rule of inference would allow us to infer 'Ha' from '(x)Hx'. It would also allow the inference of '(y) ((Ac & Cy) → Scy)' from (3b). That is, we could infer from (3b) that each thing y is such that if Callias is an Athenian and y is a Cretan, then Callias is smarter than y.

To specify an adequate set of rules is too lengthy a task to be undertaken here. Here are the important points to note about rules of inference: Following these rules allows us to infer from a set of sentences (premises) another sentence (a conclusion), with the guarantee that if the premises are true, the conclusion is true. That is, if an argument is constructed so that the conclusion follows according to the rules of inference, we are assured that the argument is valid. Specifying the rules of inference gives content to the phrase 'follows logically'. To assert that a sentence Ψ follows logically from a sentence Φ is to assert that a string of sentences can be exhibited, beginning with Φ and ending with Ψ, such that each member of the string follows from one or more of the preceding members according to a rule of inference.

We are now in a position to state, very briefly, part of what is involved in constructing a predicate calculus.

To establish such a system of symbolic notation, we must first specify a vocabulary and give the rules for constructing sentences using this vocabulary. This involves listing those symbols which can be used as individual constants, one-place predicate symbols, two-place predicate symbols, and so on. Then rules are devised that state which strings of symbols are to be allowed as *well formed*—that is, which ones are of a form that makes sense (such as 'Wc') and which are not (such as 'c∃W'). Second, the rules of inference are given. As noted above, they specify how one sentence can be inferred from another sentence or set of sentences.

It is important to note that these rules may be specified without any reference to the notion of truth or to English words for which the symbols stand. That is, we may consider how a sentence such as 'Wc' can be combined with other sentences, what its role is in various arguments, and whether or not it is well formed, without taking it to stand for some English sentence and without considering its truth or falsity.

Such rules are called *syntactical*. Syntax is the study of the forms of certain groups of symbols abstracted from any questions about their content. In the preceding sections, we have closely related our remarks about logic to the English language—even introducing the symbols '&' and '∨' to represent 'and' and 'or'—because the important use of logic for our purposes is in symbolizing English sentences and determining the validity of arguments. But it should be emphasized that logic proper is independent of any particular natural language.

This should not be taken to suggest that logic is concerned only with syntax. Systems of deductive logic are developed with constant attention to the goals of preserving truth and not introducing information into the conclusion that is not contained in the premises of an argument. Further, connectives are not just meaningless marks; for example '&' is given a meaning by the truth table for conjunction. Logic may be usefully thought of as the study of syntactical devices for capturing concepts such as truth and validity. These concepts, among others, which are related to questions of meaning, are called *semantic* concepts. (See Chapter III, section 1, on syntax, semantics, and pragmatics; and see Chapter IX, section 5, on logic and section 8 on philosophy of language.)

Often a formal system of logic is used to study a particular language or segment of language. In that case we must specify, in addition to the above rules, certain informal schemata of translation from the formal language to the natural language. (For example, in English one must specify that 'W' stands for 'is wise'.) And further, we must specify a universe of discourse and indicate what the constants denote.

With such rules in hand, we have at our disposal a powerful tool for revealing the truth conditions of many sentences as well as for the analysis of many arguments and concepts. Many philosophers argue that our understanding of a sentence or an argument in a natural language such as English is sharpened if we can express the sentence or argument in a language such as that of the predicate calculus. For sentences in the predicate calculus bear their form on their surface. Whether the form of a sentence in the predicate calculus is in fact the form of an English sentence of which it is alleged to be a translation depends on the adequacy of the translation. But the reader is encouraged to use the discussion in this section and in the preceding chapter as an aid to understanding the meaning and truth conditions of symbolic sentences that he or she may encounter in the course of further study.

2. Sets

The notion of a set is, intuitively, the notion of a collection of things of one sort or another. Words often used synonymously with 'set' are 'class' and 'collection'. Examples of sets are:

> the set of all wise men,
> the set of chessmen owned by Jones,
> the set of kangaroos over twenty feet tall,
> the set of all positive odd integers.

The examples illustrate that sets may have a finite or an infinite number of members and that the members may be concrete physical objects or abstract entities like numbers. Note that even though the members of a particular set may be physical objects, the set itself is not another physical object but an abstract entity. Note also that a set may be empty; that is, it may have *no* members. Such is (as far as we know) the set of kangaroos over twenty feet tall.

The Greek letter '∈' is used to represent 'is a member of' (or 'belongs to'). Therefore, 'a ∈ B' is to read 'a is a member of (the set) B'.

If we wish to enumerate specifically the members of a set, we enclose the names of its members in braces; thus, '{1,2,3}' names the set composed of the integers 1, 2, and 3. If $B = \{1,2,3\}$, it is true that $1 \in B$. The number 4, however, does not belong to B; and this may be indicated by writing '4 ∉ B'—that is, '∉' represents 'does not belong to'.

We can employ some of the symbols and concepts of predicate calculus by observing that there is a close connection between sets and properties. An object has a certain property if, and only if, the object is a member of the set of objects having that property. The set of all Athenians can, therefore, be characterized as the set of all x such that x is an Athenian (Ax). Call this set 'Θ' (theta); we write:

$$\Theta = \{x \,|\, Ax\}.$$

(Here '$\{x \mid Ax\}$' is read 'the set of all x such that x is an Athenian'.) We know that $c \in \Theta$ (where 'c', as above, denotes Callias).

Many sentences that can be translated into the notation of predicate logic can be equally well symbolized using the notation of set theory. 'All Athenians are wise' may be written, for example:

$$(1) \ (x) \ (x \in \Theta \to x \in \Omega),$$

where $\Theta = \{x \mid Ax\}$ and $\Omega = \{x \mid Wx\}$. A partial English translation of (1) is:

For all x, if x belongs to the set of Athenians, then x belongs also to the set of those who are wise (where 'x' ranges over human beings).

Two sets, A and B, are identical if and only if they have *exactly the same members*. Symbolically:

$$A = B \leftrightarrow (x) \ (x \in A \leftrightarrow x \in B).$$

In a trivial sense, A is identical to A, since it is obviously true that:

$$(x) \ (x \in A \leftrightarrow x \in A).$$

We speak of a set A as being a *subset* of another set B when every member of A is also a member of B. We use the symbol '$\subseteq$' for 'is a subset of'. Symbolically:

$$A \subseteq B \leftrightarrow (x) \ (x \in A \to x \in B).$$

Thus, $\{1,2,3\}$ is a subset of $\{1,2,3,4\}$, but the converse is not the case. In a trivial sense, any set A is a subset of itself, since for any set A it will be true that:

$$(x) \ (x \in A \rightarrow x \in A).$$

Thus $\{1,4,7\}$ is a subset of $\{1,4,7\}$. We now introduce the notion of a *proper subset*, so as to distinguish between those subsets of a given set A that are not equivalent to A, and A itself. We introduce the symbol '$\subset$' for 'is a proper subset of'. Thus:

$$A \subset B \leftrightarrow [(x) \ (x \in A \rightarrow x \in B) \ \& \ \sim (x) \ (x \in B \rightarrow x \in A)].$$

We may say, for example, that the set of husbands is a proper subset of the set of men and is equivalent to the set of married men.

As mentioned above, a set may be empty—i.e., have no members. Then, trivially, if sets θ and Ω are empty, they have the same members and hence are not two sets, but one (i.e., $\theta = \Omega$). Therefore there is just one empty set and it is called the *null set*. It is usually designated by 'Λ' and is characterized as follows:

$$\Lambda = \{x \, | \, x \neq x\}.$$

Since there is no object x that is not identical with itself, nothing satisfies the condition $x \neq x$; and the set Λ is empty (null).

Since every object satisfies the condition $x = x$, we can characterize the *universal set* 'V', which contains everything:

$$V = \{x \, | \, x = x\}.$$

Sometimes two different sets have some elements in common. For example, {1,2,3,4,6} and {2,4,5} have 2 and 4 in common. The set {2,4} of common elements is called the *intersection* of the two original sets. The intersection of θ and Ω is designated $\theta \cap \Omega$ and is characterized as follows:

$$\theta \cap \Omega = \{x \mid (x \in \theta \ \& \ x \in \Omega)\}.$$

Sometimes we are interested in all the elements that are in either of two sets. In the above example, those elements are 1, 2, 3, 4, 5, and 6. The set containing them is called the *union* of the two original sets. The union of sets θ and Ω is designated $\theta \cup \Omega$ and is characterized as follows:

$$\theta \cup \Omega = \{x \mid (x \in \theta \lor x \in \Omega)\}.$$

Now let us reconsider the universal set, introduced above. This reconsideration will lead us to one of the most striking discoveries in modern logic. If V contains *everything*, then it contains itself. A few other sets have this peculiar feature of being members of themselves, for instance, the set of all sets. Formally, a set θ has this peculiar feature if and only if $\theta \in \theta$. Let us consider all those sets that do *not* have this feature; that is, all those sets that are not elements of themselves. For example, {1,2,3} is not a member of itself. Such sets satisfy the condition: $\theta \notin \theta$. And the set R of all such sets may be characterized:

$$R = \{\theta \mid \theta \notin \theta\}.$$

In other words, R is the set of all those sets which satisfy the condition $\theta \notin \theta$, that is, those sets which do not contain themselves as members. Now consider: Does R contain itself? Assume it does. Then R ∈ R. Therefore R does not satisfy the condition θ ∉ θ and hence is not in R. In other words, R does not contain itself, contrary to the assumption. We must reject the assumption if it leads to its own denial. Let us then assume instead that R does not contain itself. Then R ∉ R; and R satisfies the condition θ ∉ θ and is therefore a member of the set of all sets that satisfy the condition. In other words, R ∈ R, contrary to assumption. This paradox was first discussed in print by Bertrand Russell and is known as *Russell's paradox*. It has profound importance for logic and the foundations of mathematics. It also serves as a dramatic illustration of the point that what seems simple and clear on the surface is often agonizingly difficult to understand on closer and more sophisticated examination. In this instance, it seemed easy enough to talk about the set of all sets that do not contain themselves. Yet that idea leads to paradox, and we can no longer be so confident in our ability to understand what seems to be a straightforward description of a set.

Exercises

1. Find an example of a deductive argument in a newspaper, magazine, or textbook and indicate the premises and conclusion.

*2. Symbolize the following sentences, providing a scheme of abbreviation for each:
   a. If John is a tall guard, then either Smith is shorter than Dokes or the coach is mistaken.

    b. Joe goes just in case the sun shines.

    c. The vice-chairman goes just in case the chairman is absent.

    d. Every philosopher thinks about some problem.

    e. No one is at home.

    f. All logicians are acute or I have been misled.

*3. Consider the following sentence and scheme of abbreviation:

Gerry is an adroit surgeon and Gerry is a clumsy potter.

              A (1): (1) is adroit

              C (1): (1) is clumsy

              S (1): (1) is a surgeon

              T (1): (1) is a potter

                g: Gerry

What reasons would you offer against the following as a proposed symbolization of this sentence?

$$Ag \ \& \ Sg \ \& \ Cg \ \& \ Tg$$

4. Is it reasonable to infer 'Ma' from '(x) (Hx → Mx)' and 'Ha'? Why?

*5. On the basis of the scheme of abbreviation:

       L (*1*) (*2*): (*1*) is larger than (*2*),

translate the following sentences into English. For example, using this scheme of abbreviation, we may obtain these translations:

    (x) (y) Lxy: Everything is larger than everything.

    (∃x) (y) Lxy: Something is larger than everything.

    a. (x) (∃y) Lxy

    b. (x) (∃y) Lyx

    c. (x) (y) Lyx

    d. (∃x) (y) Lyx

e. (∃x) (∃y) Lxy
f. (∃x) (∃y) Lyx
g. (∃y) (∃x) Lxy
h. (∃y) (∃x) Lyx

6. A = {1,2,4,3}
   B = {1,2,3,4}
   Are A and B identical?

*7. List all the subsets of {1,2,3}.

8. Explain briefly why it must be the case that:
   a. (Ω) (Λ ⊆ Ω)
   b. (Ω) (Ω ⊆ V)

III

Further Logical Notions

1. Important Terms

What follows are some remarks about the meanings and uses of a few key words and phrases which occur sufficiently often in philosophical writings to deserve special attention. These words are discussed here because, although they are often used outside the context of logic, they constitute an important part of the technical vocabulary of logical analysis.

SYNTAX, SEMANTICS, AND PRAGMATICS

Languages such as English and German contain many words; languages such as Cantonese and Japanese contain many ideograms; and languages such as that of the predicate calculus mentioned in Chapter II contain many signs that stand for other linguistic expressions. Philosophers often speak of signs that stand for linguistic expressions as *symbols;* and words, ideograms, and symbols can all be thought of as signs of a certain kind. The study of language is often divided

59

into three substudies, following a traditional division within the theory of signs of communication.[1]

Syntax, as we suggested in the section on predicate calculus in Chapter II, deals primarily with the *forms* of groups of signs or symbols and with relations that may hold among signs or symbols. One may address syntactic questions independently of the content, meaning, or interpretation of signs, except as that meaning is exhausted by the rules that govern the introduction of the signs into a language and their interrelations within it. In formal logic, rules that provide for the construction of well-formed formulas and inference rules are syntactic rules.

Semantics is concerned with signs as interpreted. Semantics deals with questions of relations between signs and what they refer to, signify, or designate. Philosophical theories of meaning and of truth are placed within this broad subject. In formal logic, semantic questions are often studied within model theory. But even as a cursory summary, this characterization must be expanded. For even if the relation between a name and what it names seems an easy one to grasp, this intuitive ease is strained when we come to consider other linguistic expressions. Semantic relations are relations between signs or expressions and the world. We may speak of semantic relations between such linguistic expressions as 'is a house' and houses by saying that the predicate *is true of* houses or by saying that houses *satisfy* the predicate expression. For sentences, the role of the relational notion '. . . is true of . . .' is taken over by the predicate '. . . is true.'

Pragmatics is concerned with the uses of signs, as these uses

---

[1] Charles W. Morris was instrumental in propagating this usage through *Foundations of the Theory of Signs*. Chicago: University of Chicago Press, 1938. However, Morris acknowledges there that the distinction owes much to the nineteenth century American philosopher C. S. Peirce.

are made possible by the characteristics of a language rather than as they reflect the psychological or sociological position of language users. Pragmatic questions are questions about the relations among signs, their semantic properties, and their use. These are questions of how linguistic signs can be used and of what it is about a language which makes these uses possible. The discussion of indexical expressions in Chapter IV will illustrate several pragmatic questions, and recent work in formal logic also has taken up the contribution of context-dependent expressions to the formal properties of sentences. But as the discussion in Chapter IV will indicate, these three substudies are not so much independent as they are different in their respective emphases.

'LOGICAL FORM', 'FOLLOWS LOGICALLY', AND 'LOGICAL CONSEQUENCE'

In light of the above discussion, it will be instructive to reconsider some of the concepts used in Chapters I and II. In order to argue that argument (P) in the section on arguments, validity, and truth in Chapter I was invalid, we asserted that it had the same logical form as argument (O), which had true premises and a false conclusion. Using the informal account of validity that an argument is valid just in case no argument of the same form has true premises and a false conclusion, we were able to cite (O) as a counterexample to any claim that (P) was a valid argument.

The question of the logical form of a sentence is usually taken to be a syntactic one, a question of what the formal components of the sentence are and of how they are used to produce the sentence. As a syntactic question, it is to be answered in terms of the syntactic or formal elements available to us in the language in which the sentence occurs. However, questions of logical form for sentences in a natural language such as English are much more complex than questions of logical form in a language such as that of the predicate calculus. For this reason, philosophers often speak of the logical form of a sentence in a natural language in terms of the logical form of its symbolization in a formal language.

The use of the tools of formal logic to reveal the form of sentences in a natural language and to evaluate arguments in a natural language depends on our being able to capture the logical form of sentences in a natural language by symbolizing them in a formal language that can display the form common to arguments with different content. But how is one to decide when a sentence in a formal language has the same form as an English sentence?

Consider again sentences such as those discussed in Chapter II. For instance:

(1) All Athenians are wise.

We argued that the form of (1) could not be represented as

(2) (x) (Ax & Wx)

but that the form of (1) could be represented as

(3) (x) (Ax → Wx)

Our argument was not based on syntactic grounds. We did not, for example, claim that the element of our formal language ' → ' could be used to translate the English word 'are' when it occurred between predicate expressions. Nor could we have offered any such simple argument as sound.

For we also argued that the form of

(4) Some Athenians *are* wise

could not be captured by

(5) $(\exists x)(Ax \rightarrow Wx)$

Rather we argued for (3) as the better representation of the form of (1) on *semantic* grounds, claiming that the truth conditions of (3) more closely matched those of (1) than did the truth conditions of (2).

We claimed also that (1) and (2) differed significantly in their *logical consequences*. Was this a syntactic claim or a semantic one? Recalling the discussion in Chapter II, we can say that to assert that a sentence Ψ *follows logically* from a sentence Φ or that Ψ is a *logical consequence* of Φ is to assert that a string of sentences can be exhibited, beginning with Φ and ending with Ψ, which is such that each member of the string is derivable from one or more of the preceding sentences according to a rule of inference. And we said that rules of inference are syntactic rules. So this characterization of 'logical consequence' and 'follows logically' was a syntactic one.

But such a syntactic characterization of the logical consequences of (1), or any other natural language sentence, would require the existence of rules of inference for sentences in that natural language. Such rules of inference would be rules identifying those components in a natural language such as English which are formal, those components that provide the structure on which inferences depend; these rules would reveal the relations among different formal components. To be adequate rules of inference, they would have to foster the goal of logic, which was described *semantically* in Chapter I: the preservation of truth. Unfortunately, such rules of inference for a natural language are unknown. The few which have been proposed are painfully inadequate to the task of capturing all and only valid relations of logical consequence, and serious questions have been raised about whether any syntactic rules of inference can capture those relations for a natural language.

Yet we do speak of the logical consequences of natural language sentences, and the syntactic concept of logical consequence is far too narrow to account either for philosophical or for other common uses of this notion. When we speak of what follows from sentences in a natural language, we often turn to semantic arguments. We speak, for instance, of what would be true whenever a given sentence is true. And we speak of the necessary conditions for the truth of a given sentence. And we speak of the truth conditions for sentences whose consequences we are considering. So the reader can expect to encounter claims that one sentence is a logical consequence of another which are not supportable by appeal to syntactic inference rules and which are therefore more difficult to establish.

'IMPLY', 'INFER', AND 'ENTAIL'

These are three closely related words that can easily be misused. Roughly, the distinction between the first two is that *people* infer whereas *sentences* imply. If Φ and Ψ are sentences, we may say:

(1) Jones infers Ψ from Φ.
(2) Sentence Φ implies sentence Ψ.

Example (1) means in part that Jones considers it to be the case that Ψ is a consequence of Φ. But Jones can be in error; he can infer incorrectly. In contrast, Φ cannot incorrectly imply Ψ—either Ψ is a logical consequence of Φ or it is not; and to say that Φ implies Ψ is simply to say that Ψ is a logical consequence of Φ. Thus the phrase 'incorrectly implies' has no correct use.

We may characterize inference, therefore, as a relation between a *person* and two sets of sentences (premises and conclusion); to infer is to accept a conclusion on the basis of a set of premises—if one accepts the premises. ('Infer' is sometimes used in a derivative sense to mean 'conclude from the *fact* that . . .' instead of 'conclude from the *premises* that . . .'.) Examples:

(3) Jones inferred from the first three premises that *a* does not equal *b*.

(4) Jones inferred from the fact that the sun was up that it was later than 5 A.M.

Implication, on the other hand, strictly construed, is a relation between two sets of sentences. Consider:

(5) 'All Athenians are wise and Callias is an Athenian' implies 'Callias is wise'.

'Imply' is also used in a derivative sense as a relation among *facts*. Thus:

(6) The fact that Callias is an Athenian and all Athenians are wise implies the fact that Callias is wise.

Unfortunately, the picture is a little more complicated than has yet been indicated, because there is a use of 'imply' in which *people* are said to imply.

(7) The speaker implied that war was imminent.

We may take (7) to be short for 'The speaker implied *by what he or she said* that war was imminent'. But even if we construe (7) to mean that it was not the speaker but the sentences used by the speaker that implied the imminence of war, there is one further notable difference in the way 'imply' is used in (7). When we say that a person implied something, we don't always mean that what is implied is a logical consequence of what was said; sometimes we mean that, in saying what he or she said, the speaker suggested or hinted at some conclusion. In this sense, 'imply' has a meaning close to that of 'intimate'.

Reason was given in the section on propositional logic in Chapter I against supposing that the truth table for conditionals gives the meaning of 'implies'. Neither does that truth table give the meaning of 'entails'. We shall henceforth use 'entail' as a synonym for 'imply', in the sense in which sentences, not people, imply. Thus we shall take the assertion that a sentence Φ entails a sentence Ψ to mean that Ψ is a logical consequence of Φ.

'PRESUPPOSE' AND PRESUPPOSITIONS

Although the expression 'presuppose' is sometimes (perhaps misleadingly) used in much the same way as 'imply', in the clearest use of the expression it is *people* who presuppose. In this sense, 'presuppose' means to assume or to take for granted the truth of some sentence without explicitly acknowledging or recognizing that fact. Examples:

(1) When Smith argued that the senses provide us with accurate information about external physical objects, she was presupposing that such objects exist.
(2) Most ancient Greek astronomers presupposed that all heavenly bodies moved in circular paths.

It is part of the philosopher's task to make presuppositions as explicit as is feasible; sometimes those things taken most for granted are most in need of careful inspection.

This process of making presuppositions explicit cannot go on without limit, of course. No one expects a physicist to include reasons for supposing that the sun exists, in a paper on nuclear processes in the sun's corona, even though the scientist does presuppose that the sun exists.

CONTRADICTION AND CONSISTENCY

Two sentences are *contradictory* if and only if one is the negation of the other or is logically equivalent to the negation of the other. Thus 'It is raining' and 'It is not the case that it is raining' are contradictory sentences. Their conjunction, 'It is raining and it is not raining', is a *contradiction*.

The term 'consistent' is predicated of sets of sentences. A set of sentences is *consistent* if and only if no contradiction is a logical consequence of the sentences in the set. Two sentences are *consistent with* each other if there is a consistent set of which they are members. The *set* of sentences consisting of 'Callias is wise' and 'Socrates is an Athenian' is consistent.

And the *sentences* 'Callias is wise' and 'Socrates is an Athenian' are consistent with each other. The set consisting of the sentences 'All Athenians are wise', 'Callias is an Athenian', and 'Callias is not wise' is *inconsistent* because the contradiction 'Callias is wise and Callias is not wise' is a logical consequence of the set. Two sentences are *inconsistent* with each other if *every* set of which they are members is inconsistent.

NECESSARY AND SUFFICIENT CONDITIONS

(1) If Carl won the two-mile race, then Carl officially entered the two-mile race.

(2) If Carl, and only Carl, ran the two-mile race in the fastest time ever recorded, then Carl won the two-mile race.

These two sentences are chosen to illustrate the difference between *necessary* and *sufficient* conditions. The truth of 'Carl officially entered the two-mile race' is a necessary condition for the truth of 'Carl won the two-mile race'; that is, it is necessary to enter a race in order to win it. But clearly, it is not sufficient for winning a race that one enter it. Something more is required—namely, officially completing the course before any other contestant.

Consider (2). The truth of 'Carl, and only Carl, ran the two-mile race in the fastest time ever recorded' is a sufficient condition for the truth of 'Carl won the two-mile race'; that is, to win a race it is sufficient that one run the race in the fastest recorded time and be the only one to do so. But it is not necessary, because it is possible to win a particular race and still not break any record.

When two sentences are connected by 'If . . . , then . . .', the first sentence is called the antecedent and the second the consequent. We may generalize the remarks made about the example sentences by saying that the truth of the antecedent of a true conditional sentence is a sufficient condition for the truth of the consequent. The truth of the consequent is, on the other hand, a necessary condition for the truth of the antecedent. Consider sentences (1) and (2) again. The truth of 'Carl won the two-mile race', which is the antecedent in sentence (1), is a sufficient condition for the truth of 'Carl officially entered the two-mile race', since no one can win a race in which he or she is not officially entered. And the truth of 'Carl won the two-mile race', which is the consequent in sentence (2), is a necessary condition for the truth of 'Carl, and only Carl, ran the two-mile race in the fastest time ever recorded', since he could not have run the race in the fastest recorded time, and have been the only one to do so, without winning. In a true biconditional sentence, '. . . if and only if . . .', the truth of either of the two sentences connected by 'if and only if' is a necessary *and* sufficient condition for the truth of the other. As an example, consider:

(3) Joel is Martha's husband if and only if Martha is Joel's wife.

'IS' AND 'SAME'

The verb 'to be' is used in at least four ways, which should be carefully distinguished.

First, note that 'is' may be used to indicate identity. The sentence 'Callias is the wisest man in Athens' may be symbolized by 'c = d', where 'd' abbreviates 'the wisest man in Athens'. That is, Callias is identical with that wisest man.

In the sentence 'Two plus two is four', 'is' again means the same as 'is identical with'.

Second, 'is' may be used to predicate some property of an object. The 'is' of predication is illustrated by 'Callias is wise'.[2]

Third, we sometimes use 'is' to indicate the unqualified existence of something, as in the sentence 'He is' (that is, 'He exists'). In this case no property is predicated of the subject; we are merely claiming that the subject exists.

Finally, 'is' may be used to indicate class inclusion. For example, 'Pleasure is good' may mean that the class of pleasant things is included in the class of good things. (See Chapter II, section 2, on sets.)

These distinctions are so straightforward that one may well wonder why they are made at all. The fact is that it is not always a simple matter to decide which way 'is' is being used, and it is sometimes easy to be misled by failing to make these distinctions. For example, the fact that 'is' can play these different roles can lead to confusion as to whether a particular statement is a factual claim or a definition. In fact, an example used above ('Pleasure is good') may in some contexts be correctly interpreted as utilizing the 'is' of identity and in other contexts be correctly interpreted as utilizing the 'is' of predication. Occasionally philosophers may not be clear themselves as to which of these possible claims they wish to assert. They may then use several different

---

[2] That the predicative use of the verb 'to be' is further complicated may be seen by considering the following examples:

(1) Condors are large.

(2) Condors are becoming extinct.

If we assume that both of these sentences exemplify the same predicative use of 'are', we must conclude that the properties of being large and of becoming extinct are attributed to different kinds of objects. For although an individual condor may be large, no individual condor can become extinct.

arguments, each of which would be support for a different claim, to support what appears to be one claim.

The word 'same' suffers from an ambiguity similar to that of 'is'.

Consider as an example the sentence 'This is the same card that I drew in the cut last night'. 'Same' here may indicate that there is only one card referred to—in other words, that the deck used last night is the deck being used now, and the card drawn last night is identical with the card now drawn. But 'same' could also indicate that the card drawn now is indistinguishable in respect to some specifiable (though in this case unspecified) criteria such as rank and suit. The distinction being made here can be clarified by giving two different paraphrases, which utilize the notion of a set:

(1) The card I have now drawn is a member of all and only those sets of which the card I drew last night is a member.

(2) There is a set of card kinds (for example, the set of fives of spades) of which both the card I have now drawn and the card I drew last night are members.

In using 'same' in this second sense, to indicate that two things belong to the same set, it must be clear what the relevant characteristics are in virtue of which the objects are said to belong to one set. The context of discussion will usually make this clear. For example, the claim that all brands of aspirin are the same would generally be taken to mean that in respect to such characteristics as relieving pain, reducing fever, and so forth, they are all about equally effective but not that they are alike in respect to retail price or annual advertising budget.

But it is often the case that it is not at all clear what is meant by a statement of the form 'A and B are the same' or 'A is like B'. This imprecision of 'same' and 'like' is emphasized in riddles such as the Mad Hatter's famous question, 'Why is a raven like a writing-desk?' Unfortunately, some philosophical statements turn out to be riddles when they are not intended to be.

'MUTUALLY EXCLUSIVE' AND 'JOINTLY EXHAUSTIVE'

The phrase 'mutually exclusive' expresses a relation that holds between any two sets just in case no member of either set is a member of the other. In an extended sense, the sets in a given collection of sets can be said to be *mutually exclusive* if and only if no two sets in the collection have any member in common. Thus the set of even positive integers and the set of odd positive integers are mutually exclusive because there is nothing that belongs to both sets.

In any particular application of the concepts and techniques of set theory, we have in mind a collection of objects that can be members of the sets with which we are concerned. That is, if we are discussing real number theory, we will be interested in sets whose members are real numbers. Or we may be discussing sets whose members are men, factories, and so on. In each case, we can specify a *domain of discourse*— a collection of entities from which may be drawn the members of the particular sets under discussion. The sets in a given collection of sets are said to be *jointly exhaustive* (with respect to a specified domain of discourse) if and only if every member of the domain is a member of one or more of the sets in the collection.

If we take as the domain the set of positive integers, then the two sets of odd and even integers mentioned above are jointly exhaustive. If our domain is the set of positive real numbers, then those two sets are not jointly exhaustive, because the number π, for example, is a positive real number but not an integer.

The sets in a collection of sets may be jointly exhaustive without being mutually exclusive and vice versa.

As a final illustration, let the domain of discourse $\mathfrak{D}$ be specified by:

$$\mathfrak{D} = \{A,B,C,D,E\}$$

(1) The sets $\{A\}$, $\{B\}$, $\{C\}$, $\{D\}$, $\{E\}$ are mutually exclusive and jointly exhaustive.
(2) The sets $\{A,B\}$, $\{B,C\}$, $\{D,E\}$ are jointly exhaustive but not mutually exclusive.
(3) The sets $\{A\}$, $\{B\}$, $\{C,D\}$ are mutually exclusive but not jointly exhaustive.

We often speak loosely of properties rather than sets being mutually exclusive, meaning that no object can have both properties. For example, evenness and oddness (of numbers) are mutually exclusive properties.

UNIVERSALS AND PARTICULARS

The predicate calculus, as described above, rests on a distinction between referring expressions (such as individual constants and definite descriptions) and classificatory or characterizing expressions (such as predicates of varying complexity). This distinction is a reflection of a traditional philosophical distinction between *particulars* and *universals*.

Intuitively, a particular is any individual entity. Socrates, the number five, and the third manhole cover going east from Broadway on 42nd Street are each particulars.

Typically, our talk about particular entities consists in attributing some property to the individual in question. Thus, when we claim that the barn is red, we employ the predicate 'is red', which is (or might be) true of more than one individual. But the use of such general expressions poses the following question. How are we to account for the fact that individuals have *properties* (such as redness) in common, that they seem to share certain common *patterns* and *characteristics*, and that we can speak meaningfully of *kinds* of things? One traditional answer to this question is that, besides particulars, there exist also such common characteristics or properties; they are called *universals*. Examples of universals are redness, tallness, honor, beauty, and evenness (as attributed to numbers).

A universal may have many instances, one instance, or no instances; the concept of positive even prime number is a universal that has one instance; and the concept of unicorn is a universal that, as far as is known, has no instances. There will be a universal corresponding to each general expression, such as 'red', 'man', 'unicorn', or 'tall'. Universals, of course, are abstract entities that have no spatial extension and are not to be met in sense experience in the way that physical objects are.

The particular–universal distinction, then, is concerned with the question 'What exists?' and is separate from the grammatical distinction between singular and general terms, though closely related to it. Plato argued that universals exist and that their existence does not depend on the existence of particulars. Other philosophers have denied that universals exist while still seeking to maintain the singular term–general distinction. However the question is decided, talk of universals is so widespread in logic and philosophy that the universal-particular distinction should not be ignored.

2. *Modal Logic*

In philosophy of religion, as elsewhere, one often hears it said of some claim not merely that it is true but that it is *necessarily* true. Thus, for example, it is sometimes claimed that it is necessary that God exists. But too often such claims are obscure, and if we are to evaluate them successfully, we need a clear characterization of what such expressions as 'necessary' and 'possible' mean. Often we do not literally say what we mean, as (1) and (2) below illustrate:

(1) It is necessary that you renew your driver's license before it expires.
(2) Food, shelter, and clothing are necessary.
(3) It is necessary that either today is Monday or today is not Monday.

Consider (1) and (2). Of course, it is not literally necessary that one renew a driver's license before it expires. Consider:

(1') It is necessary that you renew your driver's license before it expires if you are to drive legally.

Sentence (1') makes explicit an understood condition, which was probably left out of (1) because it is assumed that one will desire to drive and to drive legally. Consider:

(2') It is necessary that if humans are to live comfortably they have food, shelter, and clothing.

Sentence (2') makes explicit an understood condition left out of (2) (once again, probably because it is assumed that humans wish to live comfortably). Both (1') and (2') are examples of what is sometimes called conditional necessity. But it is perhaps more important to note that (1'), (2'), and (3) illustrate three somewhat different senses of 'It is necessary that'. Sentences (1') and (2') have the form:

It is necessary that $(\Phi \to \Psi)$.

But the contained conditional is not the only reason that can be given for saying that they express conditional necessity. For (1') holds only on the assumption of certain legal conventions. It is possible for there to be states where licensing of drivers is optional. We may make this further condition explicit in:

(1") It is necessary that if the state in which you drive requires by law that each driver be licensed, then if you are to drive legally you will renew your driver's license before it expires.

Sentence (2') holds only on the assumption of certain causal conditions for comfortable living for humans. Certainly it is imaginable that there be a world in which humans need neither shelter nor clothing for comfortable living.

But (3) is not based on any assumption of conventions of causal conditions. There is no possible world in which (3) is false, for (3) is a statement of *logical* necessity. Philosophers, in so far as they are concerned with notions of possibility and necessity, are interested primarily in *logical* necessity and possibility. We shall therefore try to present a more careful characterization of these notions, bearing in mind that it is only the logical sense of possibility and necessity that this characterization is aimed at reflecting.

Let us begin by introducing '$\square$' as a representation for

'It is necessary that' and '◇' for 'It is possible that'. We shall utilize the conventions for exhibiting the logical form of complex sentences adopted in Chapter I. Symbols '□' and '◇' express *modal operators;* we can point out several interesting relations that hold between sentences that are formed using these operators:

Sentences of the form:	are logically equivalent to sentences of the form:
1. ◇Φ	1. ~□ ~ Φ
2. ◇ ~ Φ	2. ~□Φ
3. □ ~ Φ	3. ~◇Φ
4. □Φ	4. ~◇ ~ Φ

Intuitively, what line 1 says is: To say it is possible that Φ is to say it is not necessarily the case that ~Φ. Line 2 says: To say it is possible that ~Φ is to say it is not necessarily the case that Φ. Line 3 says: To say necessarily ~Φ is to say it is not possible that Φ. Finally, line 4 says: To say necessarily Φ is to say it is not possible that ~Φ.

Several interesting entailment relations between sentences of different forms can now be noted:

Sentences of the form:	entail sentences of the form:
5. □Φ	5. Φ
6. (□(Φ → Ψ) & □Φ)	6. □Ψ
7. (□(Φ → Ψ) & ◇Φ)	7. ◇Ψ
8. □Φ	8. ◇Φ
9. Φ	9. ◇Φ

Line 5 says: If necessarily Φ, then Φ. Line 6 says: If necessarily Φ and, necessarily, Φ only if Ψ, then necessarily Ψ. Line 7

says: If possibly Φ and, necessarily, Φ only if Ψ, then possibly
Ψ. Line 8 says: If necessarily Φ, then possibly Φ. Finally,
line 9 says: If Φ, then possibly Φ.

We may also use our modal operators to express the fact,
for example, that it is *contingent* that Wilt Chamberlain scored
100 points in a basketball game in 1962. For this is simply
to say that it is neither logically necessary that he has nor
logically necessary that he has not. The relationships among
modalities of necessity, possibility, contingency, and impossibility are summarized in Figure 1 for any sentence
abbreviated by 'P'.

Figure 2 represents relationships holding among modalities
and truth values. Sentences of four different kinds are
represented by the vertical lines 1, 2, 3, and 4. Modalities
and truth values are represented by the horizontal lines,
as indicated. For example:

P_1: All men are men

is represented by the line at 1. That is, it is true that P_1, it
is necessary that P_1, and it is possible that P_1. But it is not
possible that not P_1, it is not necessary that not P_1, and it is
not contingent that not P_1. Similarly, the following sentences
are represented respectively by the lines at 2, 3, and 4.

P_2: The population of Boston exceeds 50,000.
P_3: The population of North Platte exceeds 1,000,000.
P_4: The second man to arrive was the first man to arrive.

We shall now attempt to strengthen the reader's intuitions
concerning the meaning of 'It is necessary that'. Most of us
readily agree that the world might have been different than
it has been, that it could be different than it now is, and that

If it is ___ that P	we write	or equivalently	and also it is ___ that P	but it is false that it is ___ that P	and it is ___ that ~P
necessary	□P	~◇~P	possible	contingent impossible	impossible
possible	◇P	~□~P	—	impossible	—
contingent	(~□P & ~□~P)	(◇~P & ◇P)	possible	necessary impossible	contingent possible
impossible	□~P	~◇P	—	necessary possible contingent	necessary

Figure 1

79

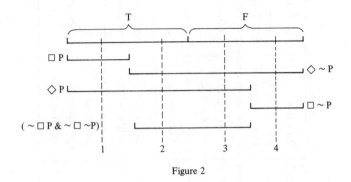

Figure 2

it could be different than it in fact will be. We can think of alternatives to the actual world as possible, though not actual, worlds. Obviously the actual world is also a possible world. It is often helpful to think of 'It is necessary that' as meaning 'It is true in all possible worlds that'. Admittedly, this suggestion will not carry us very far unless some helpful explication of the concept of a possible world can be given. But for some purposes this concept can be helpfully explicated.

We can point out two classes of sentences such that each member of these classes is true in all possible worlds. (1) Sentences that are true in virtue of their form alone (that is, all logical truths) are true in all possible worlds since the descriptive content of these sentences has no effect on their truth. (2) All sentences that are true in virtue *only* of what they mean without need to consider what the actual state of the world is are true in all possible worlds. (We assume here that the meanings of expressions in the language we are considering remain constant, regardless of what possible world is being considered.) Clearly the first set of sentences is included in this set, but this set contains sentences that are not true in virtue of their form alone. For example, 'All male siblings are brothers' and 'All red things are colored' are members of the second but not of the first class. Sentences of this second class are said to be analytically true. (See Chapter VI, section 2, on analyticity.)

These remarks based on the notion of possible worlds are intended only to aid the reader in understanding a very strong sense of 'It is necessary that' which is of considerable interest to philosophers. We have already seen that this phrase may be used when someone wishes to express a much weaker concept. Perhaps the most important points to be learned from this section are that one must be cautious in using modal language and that arguments and assertions utilizing modal language are often more difficult to understand than they initially seem to be.

Exercises

1. Which of the following sentences could be true? Explain your answers.
    (a) 'Not all men are mortal' implies 'Some man is not mortal'.
    (b) God created the world infers the world was created.
    (c) 'The world was created' incorrectly implies 'God created the world'.
    (d) John ought to return the book implies John can return the book.
    (e) The fact that John believes that he exists infers the fact that John exists.

2. What does it mean to call a set of sentences consistent?

*3. Suppose it is true that:

$$((P \rightarrow Q) \& (R \leftrightarrow P)).$$

Which of the following is true?
- (a) Its being true that P is a necessary condition for its being true that Q.
- (b) Its being true that P is a necessary condition for its being true that R.
- (c) Its being true that P is a sufficient condition for its being true that R.
- (d) Its being true that P is a sufficient condition for its being true that Q.
- (e) Its being true that R is a sufficient condition for its being true that Q.

4. Indicate for each use below of the verb 'to be' whether the use is to assert identity, predication, class inclusion, or existence. Indicate possible ambiguities.
- (a) Whatever *is*, *is* right.
- (b) Black *is* the color of my true love's hair.
- (c) Wives *are* women.

5. Discuss the following argument:
- (i) Pure-blooded Choctaw Indians are scarce.
- (ii) My great-uncle Joe is a pure-blooded Choctaw Indian.
- (iii) Therefore, my great-uncle Joe is scarce.

*6. Let the domain of discourse be {1,2,3,4}.

$$\text{Let } A = \{1,2\}$$
$$B = \{3,4\}$$
$$C = \{2,3,4\}.$$

Which pairs of sets are mutually exclusive? Which groups of sets are jointly exhaustive?

7. Discuss the following sentence with reference to the traditional distinction between universals and particulars:

   The Mona Lisa is beautiful; and surely if anything is beautiful, beauty is.

*8. Using Figure 2, indicate for each of the following sentences (A) which vertical line represents it and (B) what its truth value and modalities are:
   (a) Telephones are widely used.
   (b) Seven is greater than four.
   (c) Eisenhower was President for seventeen years.
   (d) Urban air has been polluted by industrial wastes.
   (e) Smoking cigarettes regularly is extremely unhealthful.
   (f) Most women drive sports cars.
   (g) George carved a spherical cube of wood.
   (h) Ellie's brother is her nephew's wife.
   (i) Urban air is found in cities.

9. Give two examples each of sentences that are represented by lines 1, 2, 3, and 4 of Figure 2.

IV

Truth and the Vehicles of Truth

1. Sentences, Types, and Tokens

Philosophers typically are concerned in a number of ways with questions of truth. Thus, for example, in Chapter I we discussed the relationship between the truth of some sentences (the premises) and that of some other sentence (the conclusion) in an argument. The truth tables of Chapter I are likewise a partial example of another important preoccupation of philosophers: the study of truth conditions or the circumstances in which the sentences of a language are true. Identifying what the truth conditions are for sentences of one kind or another is not the activity of investigating whether these conditions actually obtain. To know, for instance, the truth conditions for conjunctions—that a conjunction is true just in case both of its conjuncts are true—is not to know of any particular conjunction whether its conjuncts are true. So it is not to know of any particular conjunction whether it is in fact true. Still another philosophical inquiry about truth has to do with the meaning of the word 'true'. A further question one may ask is 'What is true?' But that question can be taken in at least two ways: (1) as an inquiry into what the facts about the world are—that is, an inquiry into which of the claims of physics, sociology, economics, and so forth, are true; or (2) as an inquiry into what *sorts* of things are true—that is, an inquiry into whether it is sentences, actions, assertions, or people that can have the property of being true. It is with the second question that we shall first be concerned in this section. That question is one that must be answered, for if we do not know what kinds of entity can have truth value, we may not be able to tell whether or not some questions make sense when they are of the form 'Is x true?' —for example, 'Is Smith's action true?'

The word 'true' appears in many contexts that are not of special concern to a philosopher interested in problems of truth. Consider a few examples:

(1) Joan is true blue.
(2) That material is true alligator, not a plastic imitation.
(3) My partner has always been true to me.

These examples are not of direct philosophical interest. The following conversation, on the other hand, contains a use of the predicate 'is true' in a context that may be used as a starting point for a philosophical examination of the concept of truth:

Apprentice electrician: There is no point in going back to the truck for a voltmeter. I can check it with my fingers; 110 volts isn't going to hurt me.

Journeyman electrician: That's true; but if it is 220 volts, the twenty-foot drop to the ground may be a bit jarring.

As this conversation indicates, we often use 'true' as a sort of me-too expression, a short way to say what has just been said or to agree with what has just been asserted. Thus one is tempted to say that the kind of thing that can be true or false is *assertions*. But if this answer is to provide insight into the concept of truth, we must ask what assertions are. Are they sentences, or are they actions? It is sufficient for our purposes to note that sentences and actions are indeed different sorts of things and that therefore the claim that assertions are the things that are true or false is subject to differing interpretations.

Asserting is something that people *do*; so we may say that assertions are a kind of action. But it is at least counter-intuitive to say that actions are the sorts of things that are true or false. We would not want to say that every action— for example, John's robbing a bank—was either true or false. We need a way to distinguish those actions that can be true or false from those that cannot. Thus it becomes clear that the claim that assertions are the things that are true or false is not unproblematical.

We have said that 'true' is often used to assert the same *thing* as has been said, to agree with *what has been asserted*. Perhaps we should have said that it is the product of an act of asserting—what is *asserted*—that is either true or false. Let us for the time being assume that sentences are what is asserted and thus that it is sentences that are either true or false. This seems to give a clear answer to the second question about truth, since it seems to be clear what sentences are. But consider this: How many sentences are there in the box below?

A | Peter is now thirteen years old.
Peter is now thirteen years old.

Is there one sentence there or two? Philosophers concerned
with language have settled this question by making a distinction between sentence *types* and sentence *tokens*. There are
two sentence tokens in the box, but only one type. A
written token is a collection of physical objects, in this case
bits of paper marked with ink and arranged in a specified
order with appropriate spacing. A written sentence token
is made up of word tokens (which in turn are made up of
letter tokens) and punctuation tokens. A spoken sentence
token is probably best thought of as an event, a happening,
of which people are usually made aware by vibrations in
some physical medium. Consequently, one can observe that
same written token many times, but a spoken token can
never be reduplicated. Each token is a particular object
or event.

Although the two tokens in the box are therefore different
tokens, they are obviously alike in many respects, so much so
that we may often say that there is only one sentence in the
box. The likeness of these tokens is then explained by saying
that they *instantiate*—that is, are instances of—the same
sentence type or that they are tokens of the same type. Sentence
types are not physical objects that can be located in space
and time; thus it was misleading to say that there is one
sentence type *in* the box. There is only one sentence type
instantiated by the sentence tokens that are in the box. The
same sentence type may also be instantiated in handwriting
or in italic type, and it might be instantiated orally; thus two
tokens can differ a great deal and still instantiate the same
type. What is required for two tokens to be of the same type is
that they be composed of the same words in the same language
in the same order. Nonetheless, just how much two tokens
can differ while instantiating one type is not always clear.

But if it is sentences that are either true or false, is it

sentence types or sentence tokens? If it is sentence types that can be true or false, we might say that the type instantiated by the token 'Peter is now thirteen years old' is true only at the time when Peter is actually thirteen years old. But fixing the type that a token instantiates does not fix the reference of the terms in the token; that is, we do not know to whom the name 'Peter' refers, nor do we know automatically what time is referred to by 'now'.

We have already said that tokens instantiating the same type may differ from one another in many ways; clearly they may be spoken or written at different times and by different people. Different tokens instantiating this same type may be used to refer to many different persons named Peter, only some of whom will be thirteen years old, and they at different moments of time. Suppose tokens of this type appeared last year on the medical chart of Peter Smith, who was then thirteen years old, and today on the chart of Peter Brown, who is twenty years old. What then would we say of the truth of the type? In one situation Peter is thirteen years old when the token is produced; in the other Peter is not. But we do not want to say that the sentence type is both true and false.

In discussing the possibility of types being true, we mentioned the idea of the reference of tokens; in fact, it was tempting to say that the token that referred to Peter Smith was true, while the one that referred to Peter Brown was false. Let us see whether sentence tokens provide a more satisfactory answer to the question of what sorts of things can be true or false.

We do not immediately face the same problem with tokens that we faced with types, since a particular token is written or uttered in a particular context, which sometimes aids in determining the reference of its terms; for example, the token written on Peter Smith's medical chart. But sometimes it is not possible to determine the reference of a particular token. Is the first token in box *A* above true or false? That token was used as an example, and as such it has no context that aids us in establishing the reference of 'Peter'.

Likewise, a token does not always help to determine the reference of 'now'. This fact is perhaps not obvious, for each token must be uttered, written, or otherwise produced at some particular time. This time can apparently serve as the reference of 'now'. Hence the context of a given token seems to provide the missing reference. A similar suggestion can be made concerning all tokens containing words whose reference depends on the time, place, or other circumstances of their utterance—that is, on the context of the token. Such expressions are variously known as *token reflexive* expressions or *indexical* expressions. Less common terms for such words or expressions are '*egocentric particulars*' and '*deictic expressions.*' They include such words as 'here', 'today', 'this', 'I', and 'you'. It might seem that their reference in a given token can always be determined contextually. Then the meaning of each sentence token containing indexicals is presumably expressible by replacing each indexical expression by one that refers to the same contextually determined time, place, object, or person.

This replacement strategy does not always work, however. If it were the whole story, there would not be much sense in asking, 'What time is it now?' 'Where are we?' 'What book is this?' or 'Who are you?' For if the indexical word in each of them were replaced by an expression specifying its objective reference, nothing would remain to be asked. An answer to the first question could, for instance, be 'The time now is ten o'clock.' If this answer is true and if the replacement program works, then this answer would be tantamount to the vacuous sentence 'The time at ten o'clock is ten o'clock.'

But an empty sentence such as this cannot be the information sought in asking such a perfectly straightforward question. Hence this line of thought fails. More generally speaking, we cannot assume that the time, place, and other circumstances of an utterance of a given sentence containing indexical expressions are well enough known to allow for a replacement of the kind just mentioned. What is even more important is that it is not true that the replacement, even when it can be accomplished, preserves those features of a token which determine its meaning.

This strongly suggests that indexical or token reflective discourse cannot be reduced to context-independent discourse. It also suggests that sentence tokens cannot be the bearers of truth and falsity. This latter suggestion is further strengthened by observing that there will be sentence types that are not instantiated by any sentence token. (We cannot give an example of one, for to do so would require instantiating it.) If only sentence tokens are true or false, then none of these uninstantiated types could be either true or false. Yet it seems reasonable to speak, for example, of mathematical truths that have not ever been explicitly expressed.

2. Propositions

At this point, it is well to reflect on the course of this discussion. Because it seemed counterintuitive to say that actions can be true or false, we were led to say that it is what is asserted—sentences—that can be true or false. And because the question of the truth of a sentence type was complicated by the fact that tokens of the same type can have different references, we turned to sentence tokens. But in addition to the difficulty that there seem to be more things true or false than there are sentence tokens, we must ask if it is any more plausible to say that these collections of physical objects or events are true or false. Isn't it rather what these things *mean* that is important in discussions of truth?

Suppose someone asserts that Φ entails Ψ and also asserts Φ, expecting us to infer Ψ. Isn't it going to be important that Φ in 'Φ entails Ψ' means the same thing as Φ in isolation? Surely something must be the same in the two cases in order that the entailment may hold. But *what* must be the same? The tokens obviously will be different, and tokens of the same type can have different truth values. We want not only tokens of the same type but tokens that mean the same thing, have the same reference, and therefore have the same truth value. Because of the importance of meanings in such considerations, philosophers have sometimes said that logical relations, such as entailment, hold among *propositions*—that is, among the meanings of sentence tokens, rather than among the tokens themselves—and that these meanings or propositions are the things that are true or false.[1]

If two English sentence tokens mean exactly the same thing, then it is said that they are synonymous and express the same proposition. For example, we may say that 'Not every dog is white' and 'It is not the case that every dog is white' express the same proposition. Whereas a single sentence type can be instantiated by tokens that have different meanings, a single proposition can be expressed by different tokens only

---

[1] We do not directly discuss the claim that it is statements which are either true or false, since the word 'statement' has been ambiguously used in philosophical discussion. Statements have been taken to be acts of assertion, sentence tokens, sentence types, and propositions; but all these notions have been discussed in this section. The same remarks apply to the word 'claim'.

when those tokens have the same meaning, since the meaning is the proposition expressed. Further, one proposition may be expressed by sentence tokens in different languages. Traditionally, one reason for introducing the notion of a proposition has been to explain the possibility of translation; it is presupposed that translation is possible only if two sentences in different languages have the same meaning. If an English sentence token can be translated into German without change in meaning, then the English token and the different token that is its German translation express the same proposition. Each token, being spoken or written in a particular language, is bound to that language; but propositions are not bound to any *particular* language.

Propositions are sometimes said to be timeless. That is to say, if propositions are what is true or false and if some particular proposition is true now, then it always has been and always will be true. Note that while any one written token may instantiate only one sentence type, it may express more than one proposition at different times. Imagine that Jack plays a practical joke on Jill and sends her literally the same postcard with the message 'I wish you were here' from two different places on two different occasions. (After its first arrival, he removed it from her desk when he noticed that its stamp had escaped cancellation.) Imagine also that he is sincere the first time but not the second.

If propositions are what is true or false, then one and the same token may be said to express a true proposition on the first occasion and a false one on the second. On the other hand, if tokens are what is true or false, we shall have one token that is both true and false, but at different times. We may say that the truth value of the token has changed, but this change has been made possible only by the fact that the token expresses first one proposition, then another. The truth values of the propositions expressed, however, have not changed.

Yet there are difficulties inherent in asserting that it is propositions that are either true or false, because the concept of a proposition is not entirely precise. It is not surprising that these difficulties should be especially acute in the case of sentences containing indexical words. We have said that a proposition is the meaning of a sentence and that the sentence *expresses* the proposition. But consider the sentence 'It is cold out today'. If we say, once in winter and once again in summer, 'It is cold out today', then presumably what we have said in the winter is true and what we have said in the summer is false. Yet the sentence seems to have the same *meaning* in both cases. If we suppose that (1) the meanings are the same, (2) the propositions expressed are the meanings, (3) the truth values apply to the propositions, and (4) they do so timelessly, while (5) whatever is true is not false and whatever is false is not true, then we seem to be forced to say that the proposition expressed by 'It is cold out today' is true and also not true. But this is a contradiction.

We can try to avoid this problem in several different ways. We could deny that propositions are meanings after all. But then we would have to regard meanings and propositions as distinct entities, thereby raising problems concerning the relations between the meaning of a sentence and the proposition it expresses. The denial that propositions are meanings offers no insight into the claim that it is propositions that are either true or false.

We could instead hold the view that propositions are meanings but deny that the meanings are the same in the two cases referred to above. This is, in effect, the line taken by many recent and contemporary philosophers, probably by the majority of them. But it leads to considerable difficulties. In order to reach the proposition or meaning from the token given to an audience in the first place, one has to carry out an elimination of indexicals in favor of explicit specification of the relevant contextual factors. It was argued earlier that this task is hopeless. So we must regard the idea of timeless propositions as the bearers of truth values as highly suspect, even if it has enjoyed noticeable popularity. In addition, this line of thought is open to the objection that only because the sentence 'It is cold out today' has the same meaning, whether it is spoken in summer or winter, it is false in 100° summer heat but true in 20° winter cold. That is, if the sentence had one meaning when spoken in winter and a different meaning when uttered in summer, it might express a true proposition on both occasions. On either of these proposed alternatives, we are still faced with the task—in general a troublesome one—of identifying the proposition expressed by a given sentence.

But why should we assume that propositions are timeless? If we denied (4) instead of (1) or (2), we would have a simple way out of our problems. Propositions are still the meanings of sentences; they can still, for instance, be invoked to explain how translation is possible. But they are not timelessly true or timelessly false.

Why were we led to think of propositions as timeless? In discussing the question of what sort of thing is true, we have found ourselves faced with the contradictory claim that something is both true and not true. This seems to be a difficulty analogous to the one we face when we recognize that a fence that is white can be painted black all over, that whatever is black all over is not white, and that nothing is white and not white. The obvious solution to this difficulty is to recognize that the same thing can be white at one time and not white at another time. Why have philosophers been so reluctant to apply this simple solution to our present problem? The answer to this question is of considerable interest to a historian of philosophy and to a historian of thought, who will find that most of the ancient Greek philosophers adhered to a solution of this general kind. Why modern philosophers have often taken a different line and preferred to tie their propositions to a context-independent framework is not obvious, and there may well not be a single reason. It is sufficient for us here to notice that we have no objection to saying the fence has been changed when it is painted; but we saw that one sense that can be given to the claim that propositions are timeless is that propositions do not change in truth value.

A possible solution to our problem seems to be to take sentence types as true or false but add that they are not *simply* true or *simply* false; rather they are true at some specifiable time and in some specifiable place for some specifiable speaker addressing some specifiable audience. For instance, it is not contradictory to assert both that sentence type S is true at time t_1 for speaker p_1 and that sentence type S is false at t_2 or false at time t_1 for speaker p_2. Of course, we cannot rest content with this solution unless all problems of reference are solved. (Consider the discussion earlier in this section with respect to 'Peter is now thirteen years old'.) For natural languages as opposed to formal languages, this is no simple task. It should be emphasized that this sort of relativization of the concepts of truth and falsity to time and speaker lends no credence whatsoever to the mistaken doctrine that what is true depends on what someone believes is true or wants to be true.

The question of just what sorts of things are true and false has not been settled here. We shall follow the practice of speaking simply of sentences as true or false. But it must be remembered that although this manner of speaking is here adopted for the sake of simplicity, the question of the vehicles of truth is a complex one indeed.

Fortunately, this uncertainty does not affect some of the most important uses of the concept of truth in philosophical analysis. Many such uses are based on the ways in which the truth value of a complex (be this complex a sentence type, a sentence token, or a proposition) depends on the references and truth values of its components. These dependencies are usually the same no matter what we think of as the vehicles of truth. For instance, the truth-table method outlined in Chapter I is not affected if we think of the entries heading the several columns of a truth table as representing sentence tokens or propositions instead of sentence types.

By examining such dependencies of truth values on the references of component expressions, we may hope to formulate truth definitions for different kinds of sentences—that is, rules determining step by step the situations in which a sentence of a given kind is true. Such truth definitions would amount to making explicit what we discussed as truth conditions for sentences. For certain types of formal languages, such truth definitions were set forth and studied by the Polish-American logician Alfred Tarski in the 1930s. Subsequently others have extended his approach in different directions, especially to modal logics (see the discussion in Chapter III, section 2) and to natural languages. It remains controversial, however, to what extent truth conditions always operate from inside out, from simpler components to more complex components, as, for example, the truth conditions given by truth tables do. If not, truth definitions cannot be formulated in terms of step-by-step clauses which show how the truth or falsity of a sentence depends on its components.

But even if it should be shown that these simple truth definitions cannot be extended to many of the sentences that interest us, it would not follow that the truth conditions of these sentences would be either uninteresting or beyond philosophical analysis. What would follow is that viable truth conditions for significant groups of sentences are more complicated than many philosophers and logicians first thought.

Exercises

1. Give examples of two tokens of the same type.

2. Give one reason against taking sentence types as true or false.

3. What is the relation between propositions and sentence tokens?

*4. Illustrate two tokens of different types that express the same proposition.

V

Extensions Versus Intensions

1. Reference and Extensions

In section 2 of Chapter II it was noted that what can be expressed in the notation of predicate logic can usually be expressed also in the notation of set theory. This observation illustrates an important virtue of the predicate logic notation. The way in which this notation functions can be understood by speaking only of what its various expressions *stand for* or *refer to*. (This is made clear by a translation into the language of set theory, for the set theoretical notation is not only a language or notation, but embodies, as its very name shows, a theory of the objects this language can be used to speak of.)

What an expression stands for or refers to is variously known in philosophical parlance as its *extension, denotation,* or *reference*. These extensions or references are typically entities of the kind that set theory deals with. For instance, the reference or denotation of a name is its bearer; that is, the object it names. The reference of a description is likewise the object described. The extension or reference of a predicate 'Wx' with one argument place is the set specified by this predicate, which in our set theoretical notation can be expressed as $\{x \mid Wx\}$.

Following the famous German logician and philosopher Gottlob Frege, we shall also say that the extension or reference of a sentence is its truth value, *true* or *false*. Expressions having the same extension are said to be *extensionally equivalent*. Part of the cash value of saying that the way predicate logic notation operates can be understood in extensional terms is seen from the following important observation. Consider any expression in the predicate logic notation. It has an extension (reference), and so do its component expressions. If any such component expression is replaced by an extensionally equivalent one, the extension of the whole expression remains unchanged. In this sense, the extension of the expression depends only on the extensions of its component parts, not on the other features of these parts.

For instance, the extension of the sentence (Wa & Aa) is its truth value, which we have seen to be *true* if and only if both the predicates expressed by 'W' and 'A' are true of the reference of 'a'. Clearly this truth value remains unchanged if 'a' is replaced by a name or description that refers to the same object—in other words, is extensionally equivalent with it. Likewise, the truth value remains the same if 'W' or 'A' is replaced by another predicate symbol or by a predicate, as long as the replacements have as their extension the same set as the predicate letter they are replacing.

Shakespeare says that a rose by any other name smells equally sweet. Taking his cue from the Bard, one contemporary philosopher has proposed to call 'Shakespearean' any contexts in which extensionally equivalent expressions can be arbitrarily interchanged without affecting the extension of the expression which constitutes the context. A more common term for contexts of this kind is '*extensional*'.

Often philosophers require more of extensional contexts than the invariance of their extensions with respect to extensional equivalents. It is not fully clear what these further requirements are supposed to be. The intuitive motivation on which they are based is nevertheless apparent. The idea underlying the notion of extensionality is that *all* that an expression does in an extensional context is to pick out its extension and stand for it. For instance, all that a name is supposed to do is to stand for its bearer—that is, its reference. Contexts in which this is true of all names and other individual constants accordingly are often called *referentially transparent* or *purely referential.* Contexts in which our names or other individual constants do something else, or something more, than just to refer to their extensions are often called *referentially opaque.*

Referentially transparent sentences are characterized by the validity of what is known as *Leibniz' law,* also known as the law of the *subsitutivity of identicals.* It says that expressions referring to the same individual (same object) can be substituted for each other *salva veritate,* that is, without affecting the truth value of the sentence.

The following simple inference, authorized by the rules of inference of the predicate calculus, illustrates the substitutivity of identicals:

(1) The dog bites Jim.
   Jim is Joan's only son.
   Therefore, the dog bites Joan's only son.

Leibniz' law is obviously a special case of the general property of extensional contexts mentioned earlier, namely, the property that any exchange of extensional equivalents preserves extensional equivalence. At the same time, it illustrates the close connection between the references of names, and other expressions for particular objects, on the one hand and the

truth values of sentences on the other. This connection helps
to motivate our adherence to Frege's terminology in identifying the extensions of sentences with their truth values.

As was already noted, more has to be required of extensional
sentences than the validity of the substitutivity of identicals.
Another law that has to be valid if a sentence is to count
as extensional in the intended sense described above is
existential generalization. This law says, roughly but sug-
gestively, that whatever is true of a particular individual object
must be true of some object or other. By reference to the
notation of predicate logic we can say that one obtains a true
sentence if one takes any true sentence containing a name or
description, replaces this name or description by an individual
variable not occurring in the sentence—say, 'x'—and prefaces
'(∃x)' to the sentence. For instance, if 'Ws' abbreviates
'Socrates is wise' and if this sentence is true, then '(∃x)Wx'
is also true; that is, it is also true that something or other
is wise.

This law seems to be beyond all reasonable doubt.
However, its intuitive appeal depends crucially on the assumption that the function of names and descriptions is to
pick out (refer to) ordinary, commonplace objects and to do
nothing more than this. Later we shall see that this assumption is not always satisfied.

The plausibility of the law of existential generalization also
depends on the way it is formulated in ordinary language
terms. In fact, the rough English formulation just given is
much more plausible than its apparent codification in the
form of a rule of inference in predicate logic.

What is to be required of a sentence for it to be extensional
depends naturally on the kind of expressions it contains. For
instance, consider a sentence containing sentential connectives.
A number of such connectives were characterized in Chapter

I, section 3, by means of their truth tables. Now we can see that all sentential connectives that can be defined by means of truth tables are extensional; that is, they create extensional contexts. Conversely, a sentential connective is extensional only if it is truth functional. Thus we can see one reason for the interest in the truth-table technique for studying sentential connectives: It gives us a complete theory of extensional sentential connectives.

Because of the extensionality of the predicate logic notation, this notation is felt by many philosophers to be especially well understood. Accordingly, some of them have proposed to use predicate logic as their *canonical notation*—in other words, as their basic language to which they have strived to translate or otherwise reduce as much other discourse as possible. The claim that such a reduction is always possible is a strong form of the *extensionality thesis*. In its general form the thesis says that all we need in the last analysis is an extensional language. The notation of predicate logic offers us a clear, simple, and yet in many ways quite powerful language which satisfies all the wishes of an extensionalist.

In view of such sweeping claims as the extensionality thesis, it is of interest to realize that many expressions in natural languages create referentially opaque contexts. Moreover, such expressions are vital for the purpose of discussing many central philosophical concepts. Consider, for example, the distinction between voluntary actions and actions that are not voluntary. As Aristotle noted, this distinction is important because praise and blame are bestowed only on voluntary actions. Does the adverb 'voluntarily' create an extensional context when applied to a clause specifying human actions?

In order to answer this question, consider the sad story of Joan, who awakens to see a man climbing in through the bedroom window. She grabs a gun, shoots, and wounds the intruder. Unfortunately the climber is, unbeknownst to Joan, her beloved husband Conrad, who is returning earlier than expected from a vacation in the course of which he had managed to lose his house key. Did Joan voluntarily shoot Conrad? She admits that her action was a deliberate one: She voluntarily shot the man who was climbing in through the window. However, she insists that she did not voluntarily shoot *Conrad*. Absolutely not, she says; she did not have any idea that the intruder was Conrad.

In this claim, Joan has many eminent authorities on her side, from Aristotle's time to our own time. Yet her defense turns entirely on denying Leibniz' law. For if the law were valid, it would follow from her admission that she voluntarily shot the man climbing in that Joan voluntarily shot Conrad. For the expressions 'the man climbing in' and 'Conrad' refer by assumption to the same individual.

We can sum up this example by saying that it shows the invalidity of the following inference:

(2) Joan voluntarily shot the man climbing in.
The man climbing in is Conrad.
Therefore, Joan voluntarily shot Conrad.

For in the example just sketched, both premises of (2) are true while the conclusion would be taken to be false by most observers (and by most judges).

In an analogous way one can find counterexamples to Leibniz' law for a large number of philosophically interesting terms. Here are some examples of inferences that would be valid according to Leibniz' law but nevertheless are obviously invalid:

(3) George IV did not know that Walter Scott is the author of *Waverley*.

Walter Scott is the author of *Waverley*.
Therefore, George IV did not know that Walter Scott is Walter Scott.

(4) Oedipus wanted to marry Jocasta.
Jocasta is Oedipus' mother.
Therefore, Oedipus wanted to marry Oedipus' mother.

Violations of the law of existential generalization are perhaps not as glaring as these counterexamples to Leibniz' law. It is, however, clear that this law as well fails in many contexts. The following is one example among many similar ones to demonstrate this failure:

(5) Pat believes that the next governor of California is a Democrat and that he or she will be elected by a large majority. Therefore, there is someone of whom Pat believes that he or she is a Democrat and that he or she will be elected by a large majority.

In order to realize the failure of this inference, one need only imagine a situation in which Pat's knowledge of demographic trends, voter registration, and local voting behavior has led him to expect that only a Democrat has a chance to be elected but that any Democratic candidate will be a big winner, even though Pat has not formed any opinion about the person the Democrats are likely to nominate. In such circumstances the premise of (5) is true but its conclusion false; so its invalidity is shown.

The failure of existential generalization is particularly striking in contexts governed by verbs which take a *wh-construction* (for instance, knowing *who*, remembering *what*, knowing *why*, seeing *where*, and so on). Consider the following inference:

(6) Jane knows that Nicholas Blake is Nicholas Blake.
Therefore, $(\exists x)$ (Jane knows that Nicholas Blake is x).

The conclusion of (6) admits of a simple paraphrase in plain English. For what does it mean for Jane to know of some particular individual that Nicholas Blake is that individual? Clearly this is just what is meant by Jane's *knowing who* Nicholas Blake is. In general, the existentially quantified sentences which can occur as conclusions by existential generalization from a *knows that* sentence can be translated into English in terms of *knows* + a *wh*-clause. Such translations make even more obvious the failure of existential generalization here; for to know of some individual, whoever that individual is or may be, that he or she satisfies a certain condition is not yet to *know who* satisfies that condition.

Since many important sentences thus fail to be extensional, we need a terminology to discuss such failures. A context that is not extensional is often called *intensional*. In the case of contexts for a name or a description, the extensional-intensional distinction is usually taken to coincide with the distinction already introduced between referentially transparent and referentially opaque contexts. It was said earlier that in nonextensional contexts our expressions do something more than merely refer to their extensions. What this something more is in the many different cases of nonextensional contexts is a subject of considerable disagreement among philosophers. It has not been shown that all nonextensional contexts fail to be extensional for the same, or even closely related, reasons. The reader is cautioned, therefore, that thinking of all nonextensional contexts as intensional or as referentially opaque may suggest a closer similarity among them than will be borne out by additional study.

In some cases of nonextensional contexts we can see fairly easily what is involved. When a name is placed within inverted commas—that is, when it is quoted—it ceases merely to stand for its bearer. It also serves to call the reader's attention to itself, to the particular word that occurs between the quotes. It is not surprising, therefore, that Leibniz' law fails in contexts of quotation, as the following example shows:

(7) The author of *Alice in Wonderland* is best known as 'Lewis Carroll'.
Lewis Carroll is Charles Dodgson.
Therefore, the author of *Alice in Wonderland* is best known as 'Charles Dodgson'.

2. Meaning and Intensions

In other cases it is less clear what is involved in the nonextensionality of a context. A few philosophers have tried to reduce all other kinds of referential opacity to the referential opacity of quotation, but their attempts have not been universally accepted. A more promising line is perhaps to suggest that what happens in many interesting nonextensional contexts is that the *meaning* of the expressions occurring in the context is relevant to what happens in the context, to the extent that this meaning has to be utilized even in determining the extension of the larger expression that constitutes the relevant context. On this view what matters, for instance, in example (2) above is not only the identity of the man shot—in other words, the extensions of the terms 'the man climbing in' and 'Conrad'—but also how he is specified, that is, the meanings of the two expressions.

In so far as these meanings can be reified into meaning entities (semantic entities), we can introduce a terminology paralleling that which was explained for extensions. We can assume then that with each expression one can associate not only an extension but also an *intension*, sometimes known also as *sense* or *connotation*. In this way we reach a terminology frequently used in contemporary discussions. According to this terminology, each expression has two different entities associated with it: its extension and its intension. As the extensions of different kinds of expressions are different, so also are their intensions. The intensions of words are sometimes identified with the *concepts* expressed by these words. The intensions or senses of sentences are often said to be *propositions*. These contrasts are summarized in Figure 3.

It is important to keep in mind the relation of the terms 'extension' and 'extension*al*' to each other, and likewise for 'intension' and 'intension*al*'. *Every* expression has both an intension and an extension. Some sentences are called extensional and some others intensional, but both kinds of sentences have both an extension and an intension. The difference is mainly in the extent to which the two kinds can be understood in terms of extensions alone.

Intensions or senses are in philosophical usage objective, nonpsychological meanings, independent of what a speaker or writer happens to have in mind in using an expression. For this reason, they are to be distinguished from what is meant by such common English words as intention (with a *t*!) and intent. It is also useful to remember that 'connotation' is often used in literary theory and elsewhere to encompass almost everything that is associated by a speaker or writer with a word. The philosophical sense is ordinarily narrower and very nearly identifies connotation with intension or sense.

It is not very clear what intensions or senses are really like, and some philosophers have tried to do away with them altogether. Expressions having the same intension are said to be *intensionally equivalent.* Philosophers who have criticized intensions have often alleged as a part of their critical arguments that our criteria of intensional equivalence seem to be quite fuzzy.

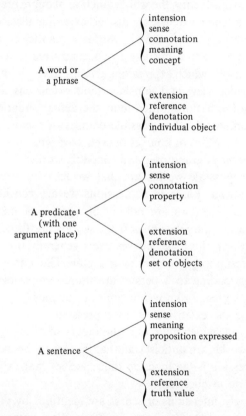

A word or a phrase
- intension
- sense
- connotation
- meaning
- concept

- extension
- reference
- denotation
- individual object

A predicate [1] (with one argument place)
- intension
- sense
- connotation
- property

- extension
- reference
- denotation
- set of objects

A sentence
- intension
- sense
- meaning
- proposition expressed

- extension
- reference
- truth value

[1] While philosophers extend the contrast between sense and reference to include multi-place predicates, the terminology surrounding the move from one-place predicates to multi-place predicates is not adequately standardized to be reflected in this chart. For example, both intensions and extensions have been called *relations.*

Figure 3

Among the other weak spots of the concept of intension there is the question as to what the relation of intensions to extensions really is. The most important theory which answers this question is the approach to meaning theory known as *possible worlds semantics*. It minimizes in a certain sense the difference between extensions and intensions. According to this theory, the whole function of our expressions is to refer to their extensions, just as extensionalists claim. However, according to possible worlds semanticists, extensionalists have made a mistake in concentrating exclusively on the extensions which expressions *actually* have. We have to take a broader view and consider their extensions also in a number of situations other than the actual situation, or under a number of other possible courses of events. These alternative situations or courses of events are what is referred to by the perhaps grandiose term 'possible worlds'.

What the possible worlds are that we have to attend to depends on what kinds of expressions we are considering. For instance, when we are talking of what someone—say, Mary—believes, the relevant possible worlds are those compatible with everything she believes. More generally, the worlds in effect presupposed in ascribing a state like knowing or hoping or intending to a person are those compatible with everything the person knows or hopes or intends.

Since it is the extension of an expression in all relevant possible worlds which matters in the theory of meaning (says a possible worlds semanticist), all that there is to the meaning of the expression is the function that specifies that extension in each world in question.

Accordingly, intensions or senses are identified by possible worlds semanticists with such functions. For instance, the intension or sense of a name is the function that specifies, for each world, the bearer of the name in that world. The intension of a sentence is the function that tells us, for each world, whether the sentence is true in that world. This function is determined uniquely as soon as the class of worlds in which the truth value is *true* is determined. Hence to speak of the function is equivalent to speaking of this class, and the intension of a sentence is therefore sometimes identified with the class instead of with the function. In either case, a proposition (being the intension of a sentence) thus receives a precise definition in possible worlds semantics.

Possible worlds semantics is a flourishing albeit controversial theory, but we cannot follow it much further here. One crucial question in evaluating it philosophically is whether alternative worlds are sufficiently realistic and knowable entities to serve as the cornerstone of meaning theory. (One logician has playfully formulated this question by asking, "Is there life on possible worlds?")

Instead of pursuing such philosophical questions, we shall register a few ways in which possible worlds semantics helps us to understand failures of extensionality. For instance, the failure of the substitutivity of identicals is clear in the framework provided by theories of possible worlds semantics. An identity '(a = b)' is true if and only if 'a' and 'b' refer to the same individual in the actual world. But the truth of this identity in the actual world does not guarantee that they refer to the same individual in other possible worlds. Hence there is no reason to expect that 'a' and 'b' should be intersubstitutable *salva veritate* (as Leibniz would say) in contexts in which we are in effect considering also such alternative worlds.

This is indeed precisely the situation in our examples. For instance in (3), we are in effect considering the different situations compatible with what George IV knew. Since he did not know that Scott was the author of *Waverley*, in some worlds compatible with what he knew 'Walter Scott' and 'the author of *Waverley*' refer to different individuals. But if so, the fact that in the actual world their references happen to coincide does not in any way justify their interchange in discussing what the king knew.

Moreover, possible worlds semantics immediately shows what extra assumptions would serve to restore Leibniz' law. These collateral premises depend on the context. For instance, in discussing what George IV knew, we are relying on the worlds compatible with everything he knew. The exchange-ability of 'a' and 'b' will hold only if they have the same extension, refer to the same individual, in each of these worlds. But according to possible worlds semantics, what it means for 'a' and 'b' to refer to the same individual in all the worlds compatible with everything George IV knew is simply that George IV knew that $(a = b)$. In other words, in a context like (3) two names or descriptions are inter-changeable only if they are known by the person in question to refer to the same individual. This restriction makes good sense intuitively; in discussing what someone believes, knows, hopes, and so on, we clearly can treat as equivalent those expressions that the person knows to refer to the same extension.

Likewise, the failure of existential generalization is readily explained by possible worlds semantics. Suppose that we are given a true intensional sentence containing a name or description 'a'. Since the sentence is intensional, it invites us (according to possible worlds semantics) to consider several different 'worlds'. In them, 'a' can very well refer to different individuals. If so, there need not be any one individual (the same individual in all the relevant worlds) of whom we can truly say what the sentence says of the bearer of 'a'. In short, existential generalization with respect to 'a' fails whenever its reference varies from one relevant possible world to another.

This is just what happens in our examples. For instance, in (5) existential generalization with respect to 'the next governor of California' fails because, under the different courses of political events Pat believes possible, different politicians will be elected. If we could make the additional assumption that Pat has a belief as to who the next governor of California is, the conclusion of (5) would follow.

These simple observations show several interesting things. First, we may note that failures of extensionality can be of several entirely different kinds. In a failure of Leibniz' law, *two* names or descriptions fail to refer to the same object in *each* alternative world. In a failure of existential generalization, *one* name or description fails to refer to one and the same object in *all* the different worlds we have to take into account. It is doubtful that much is gained by grouping such dissimilar phenomena under a single heading such as 'intensionality' or 'referential opacity'.

Another conclusion from the same observations is that only existential generalization, not the substitutivity of identicals, presupposes comparisons between the references of one and the same expression in different possible worlds. For the substitution *salva veritate* of one expression for another presupposes only that they have the same reference in each relevant world, considered alone. By contrast, existential generalization with respect, say, to 'a' presupposes that the reference of 'a' in any relevant possible world is the same as in any other. In other words, existential generalization presupposes that we can *cross-identify*, that is, that we can tell of some inhabitants of different possible worlds whether they are identical, whether they are manifestations of the same individual. This problem of cross-identification has prompted extensive discussion, and it is generally agreed to be a central issue in evaluating possible worlds semantics.

Even though we cannot survey the discussion of cross-identification in the literature, it is useful to know some of the terms in which it is couched. Manifestations or embodiments of one and the same individual in different worlds are generally known as *counterparts* of one another. It is often helpful to think of them as being connected with each other by an invisible line, the *world line* of the individual in question. (Punningly, these lines of cross-identification are sometimes referred to as trans world heir lines, or even TWAs.) A word or phrase that defines a world line—in other words, refers to the same individual in all possible worlds (or at least in all those worlds in which the word or phrase has a reference)— is often called a *rigid designator*. An older term with essentially the same meaning is *logically proper name*.

It is not obvious that there is any easily identifiable class of expressions that are always rigid designators. Examples like (6) show that grammatical proper names (in that example, 'Nicholas Blake') do not always behave like logically proper names. Indeed, at one time Bertrand Russell held that there are really only two logically proper names: 'this' and 'I'. And at a later time he argued that 'I' should be trimmed from this already meager list!

Be these problems as they may, it can be seen that a wide class of phrases can sometimes be used *as if* they were rigid designators. For instance, consider the phrase 'the next governor of California', occurring (as it did in the premise of (5)) in a context in which someone's beliefs are being discussed. Often, the phrase is taken to refer, in each world that we have to take into account, to whoever is the next governor of California *in that world*. However, the phrase can in principle be taken, as it sometimes is, to refer to one and the same individual in each of these different possible worlds, namely to the individual who *in the actual world* will next be elected governor of the Golden State. On the first reading, in determining the reference of 'the next governor of California' in an alternative world, we look for whoever is elected in that world; on the second reading we go back to the actual world, see who is there elected, and follow that person's world line to the alternative world. The former reading is known, in a terminology that goes back to the Middle Ages, as the *de dicto* reading. The use of the phrase 'the next governor of California' on which this reading is based is sometimes called its *attributive* use. The latter reading is known as the *de re* reading, and the corresponding use of the phrase as its *referential* use.

In conversational English, the *de dicto* reading of the premise of (5) might be expressed as follows:

> (8) Pat believes that the next governor of California (whoever that person may be) is a Democrat and will be elected by a large majority.

The *de re* reading may perhaps be expressed as follows:

> (9) Pat believes of the next governor of California (of the person who in fact will be the next governor) that he or she is a Democrat and that he or she will be elected by a large majority.

In (8) Pat need not have any beliefs as to who the next governor is. In (9) Pat need not identify the person his beliefs are about as the next governor. This identification is due to the speaker, not to Pat. (This point is clearer if we omit the second conjunct of (9).)

Such grammatical cues as we have in (8) and in (9) are not infallible. They are nevertheless often useful. For instance, we can now see that our first formulation of the law of existential generalization is misleading. We formulated it by speaking of what is *true of* some particular individual. This locution strongly encourages the *de re* reading, which was not the intended one. Indeed, on the *de re* reading, any phrase admits of existential generalization.

The possibility of a *de re* reading of many names and descriptions shows that the frequently used terms 'referentially transparent' and 'referentially opaque' may mislead. They are typically applied to the different contexts in which a phrase may occur. But even though the ultimate explanation of the behavior of an expression presumably depends on the context, we have seen that an expression often can be interpreted attributively or referentially in the very same context. Furthermore, different phrases occurring in one and the same context can frequently be interpreted differently, one attributively and the other referentially. Hence the 'looking through' metaphor on which the terms 'referentially transparent' and 'referentially opaque' are based is inadequate for the purpose of describing the behavior of names and descriptions in different contexts.

The word 'intentional' (with a *t*!) is sometimes used in philosophy as a technical term to refer to the characteristic features of mental acts. In this use, 'intentional' is very close in meaning to 'psychological' or 'mental', even though it is usually restricted to conscious, conceptualizable mental phenomena. The relation of intentionality, in this technical sense, to intensionality is a moot issue. We have seen that many failures of extensionality occur in contexts in which intentional or psychological phenomena are being discussed. It might therefore seem tempting to identify intentionality and intensionality. This identification would amount to the claim that the extra work our expressions do in intensional contexts is to express certain thought acts. We have seen, however, that this claim is not true of all nonextensional contexts; for example it is not true of contexts of quotations. Whether the notion of intensionality can be narrowed in some suitable way so as to rule out such exceptions remains to be seen.

Another stumbling block to any facile identification of intentionality with intensionality seems to be presented by contexts created by *logical modalities*; that is, the concepts of logical necessity and logical possibility. These seem to exhibit the same behavior as typically intensional concepts and yet do not seem to be psychological concepts. Their characteristic behavior is illustrated in the failure of the following inferences:

> (10) It is necessary that nine is nine.
> The number of planets is nine.
> Therefore, it is necessary that the number of planets is nine.

> (11) The number of planets is necessarily the number of planets.
> Therefore, $(\exists x)$ (the number of planets is necessarily x).

Here we can conclude only that the relation of intensionality to psychological (intentional) concepts requires further thought.

Exercises

1. Give an example of an extensional sentence; give an example of an intensional sentence. Establish by interchange of expressions having the same extension that the latter sentence is not extensional.

*2. What is the extension of:

    (a) 'Jimmy Carter'
    (b) 'The President of the United States of America in 1978'
    (c) 'The King of France in 1978'

3. Is the following sentence extensional? Support your answer.

    Muhammad Ali chose his name for religious reasons.

4. Express the condition for the truth of the sentence 'Ws' in terms of the extensions of 'W' and 's'.

*5. Paraphrase the following sentence to give an example of its *de dicto* and *de re* readings.

    Mark believes that the number of member nations in the United Nations is smaller than it is.

VI

The Analytic–Synthetic and
A Priori–A Posteriori Distinctions

1. *Introduction*

The distinctions to be discussed below were first systematically set forth in the eighteenth century by Immanuel Kant, but they were implicit in the works of many of his predecessors and have since been developed beyond his ideas.

It requires little reflection to convince oneself that the criteria we employ and the kinds of evidence we cite for the truth of particular claims vary markedly from case to case.

Suppose, for example, that we wish to discover whether the following claims are true:

(a) All animals are animals.
(b) The pear trees are in bloom.

In the latter case, one may well go to the place where the pear trees grow and look for blossoms, whereas the truth of the first sentence is evident merely upon an examination of its logical structure. The only evidence one might cite for (a) would be from a logic text, but the request for evidence seems out of place. The thing we do not do is go out in search of animals to see if they are animals.

To take a more interesting example, consider:

(c) God exists.

Traditionally, this claim has been supported or denied on widely divergent grounds. Some have insisted that (c) follows deductively from logically true premises, others that God's existence must be postulated to account for the world as we observe it to be, still others that because, in their view, (c) cannot be refuted or proved on the basis of the evidence of the senses, it is a meaningless claim.

Or consider:

(d) The state of sleep makes the formation of dreams possible because it reduces the power of endopsychic censorship.[1]

How would one establish the truth or falsity of (d)? The relation between this sentence and the psychoanalytic theory within which it is embedded raises several interesting questions concerning the kinds of support which can be offered for (d). Some would claim that it is a consequence, even if not a logical consequence, of some such theory. If so, one could provide evidence for it by providing evidence for the general theory, but in so doing one would not be seeking direct evidence for (d) as one might for (b). Or perhaps one should follow a procedure analogous to that suggested for (b), examining dreams and the state of sleep. But the claim under discussion involves in an essential way a theory-laden or theory-dependent concept, that of endopsychic censorship.

[1] Sigmund Freud. *The Interpretation of Dreams*. Volume 4 of The Pelican Freud Library, James S. Strachey, ed. Middlesex, England: Penguin Books, 1976 (Pelican Edition), p. 672.

It is difficult to see how one could identify the activity of endopsychic censorship independent of accepting at least certain parts of the theory that introduces it. So two quite different possibilities for providing evidence for (d) are suggested. Considered within a theory, the claim might be evidenced by showing it to be a consequence of the theory, for whose adequacy independent evidence is then provided. Considered as external to any theory, it might be the subject of investigation, if one had ways of identifying some phenomena as instances of endopsychic censorship.

In any case, discovering the truth or falsity of such claims as (c) and (d) does not seem to fit a model suggested either by (a) or by (b).

These few examples are sufficient to suggest a host of philosophically interesting questions. What criteria of truth are relevant to the claims of theology or of physics? What kinds of evidence confirm the claims of natural science or ethics or the social sciences? And how is such evidence related to the corresponding claims? What sorts of things can be known by reason alone, without reference to sense experience? And so on.

The distinctions that follow were propounded not in order to answer such questions, but in an attempt to help clarify them and make them more precise.

2. *Analyticity*

(1) $(P \& (P \rightarrow Q)) \rightarrow Q$.
(2) Queen Elizabeth II is identical with Queen Elizabeth II.
(3) A brother is a male sibling.
(4) All brothers are males.
(5) Some bachelors are married.

The foregoing sentences share this property: Their truth or falsity can be determined by an examination of their logical form and perhaps of the meanings of the words used to express them as well.

The first sentence is a tautology. The second has the logical form a = a and is thus logically true. By replacing 'male sibling' in (3) with its synonym 'brother', (3) is transformed into a logical truth. Thus the truth of (3) follows from the meanings of the words; that is, by interchanging synonyms for synonyms, we can convert (3) into a sentence whose form is obviously that of a truth of logic. The same is true of (4). Since brothers are male siblings, (4) is equivalent to 'All male siblings are males', which again has the form of a truth of logic. The meaning of the predicate in (4) is part of the meaning of the subject; (4) is a partial analysis of the term 'brother'. Finally, (5) is seen to be false once we consider the meaning of 'bachelor' and the logical form of the sentence.

Such sentences are said to be *analytic*.[2] Analytically true sentences are thus of two kinds—those [like (1) and (2)] which can be seen to be truths of logic, merely by inspection of their logical form, and those [like (3) and (4)] which can be seen to be logical truths by interchanging synonyms for synonyms and then examining the logical forms of the resultant sentences. Analytically false sentences are those that are self-contradictory. As before, synonyms may have to be

---

[2] In Chapter II, some reasons were given for claiming that propositions rather than sentences are true or false. Thus one may want to claim that it is propositions which are analytic or synthetic. This view is further motivated by the fact that criteria for analyticity depend heavily on word meanings and synonymy, so that sentences that have the same meanings (or express the same propositions) will be alike in analyticity. In this chapter, as throughout the book, we follow common usage in calling *sentences* analytic or synthetic. But, of course, the possibility remains open that it is the propositions expressed by these sentences that are analytic.

replaced by synonyms to make evident the fact that a sentence is self-contradictory.[3]

Another way to make the same distinction is to say that the denial of an analytically true sentence is self-contradictory.

All sentences that are not analytic are called *synthetic*. Some examples follow:

> (6) Queen Elizabeth II was born in 1926.
> (7) John has three brothers.
> (8) It is often the case that bachelors own sports cars.
> (9) The earth is flat.

Neither synthetic sentences nor their denials are self-contradictory. Their truth or falsity cannot be determined by word meanings and logical form alone. Crudely put, a synthetic sentence has an extralogical content, and we must look beyond the analysis of the meanings of the words involved to settle its truth value. To assert that a particular synthetic sentence is true is to assert that one of two mutually exclusive but logically possible states of affairs (described by the sentence and its denial) is actually the case.

3. *The* A Priori

Setting aside temporarily the analytic–synthetic distinction, we can divide all sentences into two groups according to whether or not they can be known to be true or false without consulting experience. Sentences of the type that can be refuted or confirmed only by experience (that is, on the basis of observation) are called *a posteriori*. They are to be

---

[3] Often 'analytic' is used for 'analytically true', i.e., often 'S is analytic' is intended to entail 'S is true'.

distinguished from sentences that can be known to be true (or false) without empirical evidence; these latter are *a priori* sentences. Thus an *a priori* sentence is such that we can conceive of nothing that would count as evidence against (or for) it. Examples of *a posteriori* sentences are easily found:

(10) It rained yesterday.
(11) It looks like rain.
(12) It will rain tomorrow.

All these are of the type of claim whose truth (or probability of being true) is to be found only by consulting our experiences.

But consider the mathematical equation:

(13) $5 + 7 = 12$

What experience will refute or confirm (13)? If we put five apples into a basket, add seven more, and then count eleven apples in the basket, has (13) been refuted or cast into doubt? Clearly not. We shall seek some physical explanation or counting error and continue to consider (13) true. Thus (13) is a paradigmatic example of an *a priori* sentence.[4]

---

[4] In ordinary discourse we often use '*a priori*' to mean 'independent of some particular experience' rather than 'totally independent of experience', as we are using it here. An example of this ordinary use is 'He should have known *a priori* that she would get angry with him for breaking the date'. That is, he should have known what her reaction would be prior to the actual *particular experience* of breaking the date.

Note too that to say that something can be known *a priori* is not to say that it can be known before any experience. Of course, we can have no knowledge of any kind before we have had experiences.

4. *The* A **Priori** *Synthetic, Etc.*

We are now in a position to construct a table illustrating
the four combinations of the above criteria and the kinds of
sentences that fall under them.

	A Priori	*A Posteriori*
Analytic	I. P or not P. All dogs are animals.	II.
Synthetic	III. Every event has a cause.	IV. Of the automobiles sold in Ohio in 1977, 18% were imported.

Clearly, there are no *a posteriori* analytic sentences (group
II) because analytic sentences are true (or false) in virtue of
meaning and form alone, so that neither refutation nor confirmation by experience is possible. Therefore, all analytic
sentences are *a priori* (group I).

Group IV comprises those sentences whose truth does not
follow from word meanings and logical form but from experience. Examples of such 'empirical' claims are, of course,
easy to find. Particular observational and predictive claims
of natural science, as well as the bulk of our everyday conversation, belong to this group.

As may be expected, the most controversial category is
group III, synthetic *a priori* sentences. Sentences of this type

are not merely analyses of words, nor are they true on logical grounds alone; they say something about the world of our experience, and yet they are known independently of empirical evidence. Leaving aside the controversy for the moment, we may justify the example given, as follows:

(14) Every event has a cause.

The negation of (14) is not self-contradictory; therefore, (14) is not analytic. And yet its truth is independent of experience because we accept no experience as a refutation of it. That is, we may be unable to find the cause of a particular event; this does not lead us to postulate, however, that it was uncaused, but merely that we are ignorant of the cause. Some philosophers have held that if Φ is any true *a priori* sentence abbreviated by 'P', then it is necessary that P. This claim is true if Φ is an analytic sentence. (See the section on modal logic in Chapter III.) If it is to be necessarily true that P for some synthetic sentence, then that synthetic sentence must be true in all possible worlds. Whether it can be that a synthetic sentence is true in all possible worlds is a point of major philosophical dispute.

Though it is sometimes asserted that the analytic–synthetic and the *a priori–a posteriori* distinctions are in reality one distinction (and that only groups I and IV are legitimate), such a view requires careful arguments for its support. The distinction between analytic and *a priori* is at least nominally clear and should not be blurred. The criterion for analyticity has to do with logical structure and word meanings, while the criterion for something's being *a priori* is its relation to evidence and experience.

Of course, even when the distinctions are clear and precise, we may have trouble deciding the status of particular sentences. As a final example, consider the following:

(15) All swans are white.

Suppose this assertion is made by a biologist soon after the discovery and naming of the species 'swan' and before black swans have yet been observed. The status of (15) may be in doubt. If it is an *a posteriori* synthetic sentence, then it is only probably true and the appearance of one black swanlike bird will refute it. On the other hand, we may take (15) as *a priori* analytic, expressing one of the properties necessary for a bird's being a swan. Then the black swanlike bird may be denied the title 'swan' and categorized as a member of a different though related species. (Or we may amend the defining characteristics to include black as well as white swans—as in fact we do.)

5. *Some Contemporary Views*

The distinctions we have been discussing help to make clear the fundamental difference between empiricism and rationalism. This difference can be set forth quite simply. Rationalists hold that there are synthetic sentences which are *a priori*, and they typically try to prove that certain basic assertions do have this status. Empiricists, on the other hand, insist that every true sentence is either analytic or else synthetic and *a posteriori*.

In the 200 years since Kant wrote about these distinctions, they have never ceased to play a significant role in philosophical inquiry. Some of the most important problems recurring in philosophy, particularly since Descartes, can be formulated directly in terms of the analytic–synthetic, *a priori–a posteriori* distinctions. In view of this, it is not surprising that much work has gone into the attempt to clarify these key concepts and to test the validity of the distinctions.

Some have asserted that there is, in principle, a fundamental imprecision in the concept of synonymy, which is fatal to the analytic–synthetic distinction. We have seen that there are two types of analytically true sentences: (a) those like 'Either today is Monday or it is not the case that today is Monday', whose truth is guaranteed by their logical form alone, and (b) those like 'Bachelors are unmarried', which can be shown to be logically true sentences by the interchange of synonyms for synonyms (in this case by the replacement of 'bachelor' with 'unmarried adult male'). Thus to show that a sentence is analytic in this second way requires that we be able to decide with precision which words and phrases are synonymous; and we must be able to pick out these synonyms independently of any recourse to the idea of analyticity. For we cannot say, on pain of circularity, that two predicate expressions abbreviated by 'S' and 'F' are synonyms if and only if '(x) (Sx ↔ Fx)' is an *analytically true* sentence. But the problem of explaining just what synonymy is then arises. The most obvious attempt at solving this problem is the suggestion that synonymous words are those that can be substituted anywhere for one another without changing the truth value of the sentences into which the substitutions are made. For example, if (16) is true, then so is (17):

(16) Charlie is an unmarried adult male.
(17) Charlie is a bachelor.

But this test will not really work. If we consider certain intensional contexts (as discussed in Chapter V), we cannot tell whether this test for synonymy has been passed unless we already know if we are dealing with synonyms. For example:

(18) Necessarily all bachelors are bachelors

is true. But our conviction that

(19) Necessarily all bachelors are unmarried male adults

is true depends on our belief that 'bachelor' and 'unmarried male adult' are synonymous. If we did not think so, we would be reluctant to call (19) true. But a test for synonymy that requires us to know already what is synonymous is of no help. Recall that our initial effort was to be completely explicit and precise about what analyticity is. That led us to consider what synonymy is, and our first attempt at answering the question failed. Other attempts have fared little better.

Those who have become impressed with the difficulty—or perhaps impossibility—of determining just which expressions are synonymous have naturally tended to be skeptical of the possibility of drawing a precise line between analytic and synthetic sentences. Of course, there are some sentences that are clearly synthetic and others whose analyticity no one would deny; but between these extremes may lie many sentences that appear to be analytic or synthetic but cannot be placed with certainty into one category or the other. It is also asserted by some that the *a priori–a posteriori* distinction stands or falls with the analytic–synthetic distinction, while others hold that the former distinction may be maintained even though the latter should be given up.

Such controversies are not yet settled, and it is not the purpose of this section to explore them further. Rather, these contemporary views have been mentioned to emphasize the fact that the definitions of 'analytic', '*a priori*', and so on, given in sections 2–4 above, are those traditionally given and are not to be taken as precise or adequate to all the work they are called upon to do. At best, what has been explained above can serve as a starting point for further inquiry; and these distinctions, though rough, can be used to shed some light on some of the perennial philosophical issues.

Another weak spot in the concept of analyticity is an ambiguity that can be found in its usual definitions. Analytic sentences are said to be true or false in virtue of their logical form and of the meanings of the words used to express them. But truth or falsity in virtue of logical form can mean either (a) truth or falsity dependent on logical form and meanings alone or (b) truth or falsity that can be seen or recognized directly from the logical form and meanings alone.

There is a significant difference between these two accounts. A broader concept of analyticity is reflected in (a) and a narrower one in (b). For what can be recognized as true on the basis of form and meanings alone surely is true on the basis of form and meanings alone. But typically we cannot recognize the truth of a logically true sentence or the falsity of a logically false one directly from its appearance, even when it is correctly expressed in a formal notation. Often considerable ingenuity is required to establish that a sentence is a logical truth. It is for the purpose of establishing logical truths which cannot immediately be recognized that many of the techniques of formal logic, with its rules of inference, have been developed.

The distinction between the narrower and the broader concept of analyticity can be illustrated through an analogy in which analyticity according to the two accounts is compared to two different kinds of theorems of elementary geometry.

Sometimes the truth of a theorem can be established by considering only the figure that exemplifies the theorem. Such theorems correspond on this analogy to analytic truths in the narrower sense. Sometimes, however, a theorem can be proved only after it has been complemented by suitable auxiliary constructions. Then the theorem does not correspond to an analytic truth in the narrower sense, but it can still correspond to an analytic truth in the broader sense. This analogy can in fact be shown to be more than a mere analogy, for the introduction of new geometrical objects in a geometrical proof through an auxiliary construction corresponds to certain steps in a logical argument which can be described intuitively as introducing new "auxiliary" individuals into the proof.

It has been claimed that the sense in which Kant was in fact using the concept of analyticity was the narrower one, not the broader. Moreover, in this sense he was correct in claiming that there are many synthetic (not analytic in the narrower sense) truths *a priori*. For many complicated logical truths can be established only by importing auxiliary individuals into the proof. Such truths are not analytic in the narrower sense, and yet they can be shown to be true through a demonstration without recourse to experience.

In contrast, many contemporary philosophers seem to have presupposed the broader sense. Yet some of them have formulated their claims as if what is true of analytic sentences in the narrower sense is true of what they are regarding as analytic. For instance, it is not uncommon to claim that logical inferences are uninformative, or at best informative only about how words and other symbols are used. It is important, therefore, to keep in mind these two senses which may be presupposed in discussions. For instance, if one conflates what is true or false on the basis of form alone with what can be recognized to be so, one will quickly be led to deny that there are truths of the former kind which are not also truths of the latter kind! But if a denial of synthetic *a priori* truths in Kant's sense is due solely to a conflation of two interpretations of analyticity, one misses the unique thrust of Kant's position and trivializes the whole question of synthetic *a priori* truth.

Some philosophers have suggested that the *a priori* element in our knowledge is, in the final analysis, of our own making, due to the ways in which we *qua* human beings come to know the world. We can know things only as having certain properties because we have, though not consciously, put those properties and relations into them in the act of coming to know them, rather as one wearing blue spectacles perceives everything as being colored blue. The spectacles wearer who is aware of the effect of the spectacles will realize that in the future, too, things will be perceived as being similarly colored unless the spectacles are removed. This kind of knowledge can be used, according to the suggestions just mentioned, as a conceptual model for our *a priori* knowledge, with one crucial difference: even if a conscious change of conceptual model is possible, it is not as easy as removal of spectacles.

As to what the properties and relations are that we are alleged to project into the objects of our knowledge and how they are imposed on objects, there is little agreement. It is not clear, either, what the relevant ways of obtaining information about the world are, or how their presuppositions are expressed in language. In any case, it is not very likely that they can all be summed up by the logical form of sentences and the meanings of the words used. If they cannot be, there will be synthetic truths *a priori* on this view too. For the truths in question are not true by virtue of logical form alone; that is, are synthetic. Moreover, these truths are not derived from experience; on the contrary, the relevant experiences may themselves be influenced by them.

Perhaps the most important tools we have for coming to know the world are different conceptual frameworks. These may, as it were, color our experience insofar as our experience is conceptualized by means of such a framework. The applicability of the framework to experience is not based on experience but is due to something prior to experience, perhaps to the way a human mind works or to our antecedent decision to adopt a particular framework. In the former case one's conceptual framework is not a matter subject to decision; in the latter it may be. Philosophers who discuss conceptual frameworks or conceptual schemes, as they are sometimes called, have not been united in respect to the possible role of choice or decision. It has been suggested that the *a priori* element in our knowledge is generated by the conceptual frameworks we are using. For instance, according to Kant, causal concepts apply to all experiences with *a priori* certainty because causality is a part of the framework that our understanding imposed on all experiences.

Sometimes sufficiently general theories are taken to play an analogous role as conceptual frameworks. Example (d) in section 1 above illustrates how the evidence for or against one of the claims made within a theory may be understood only if much of the overall theory in question is assumed to be true or true of things that actually exist. Thus theory-ladenness apparently can also create synthetic *a priori* truth of a kind.

Hence we can see that the concepts of analytic and synthetic are closely related to a number of important problems in different areas of philosophy.

Exercises

*1. Give an example of an analytic sentence, an *a priori* false sentence, and an *a posteriori* true sentence.

2. What is the criterion of syntheticity?

3. What role does empirical investigation play in the determination of the truth or falsity of an analytic sentence?

4. Can there be analytic *a posteriori* sentences? Why or why not?

*5. a. Suppose that 'gold' is defined as 'the yellow, malleable metal soluble in aqua regia'. Then what is the status of the claim that gold has an atomic weight of N? (That is, is the sentence analytic, synthetic–*a posteriori*, or what?)

   b. If we redefine 'gold' as 'that substance whose atomic weight is N', then what is the status of our original statement that gold is yellow, metallic, malleable, and soluble in aqua regia?

VII

Definition and Philosophical Analysis

1. *Definition and Explication*

A major technique of analytic philosophy is to try to formulate precisely the meanings of terms that, for one reason or another, are of special interest. This sort of philosophical activity dates back to the Greeks and their attempts to discover the nature of beauty, knowledge, justice, and goodness. Our present-day efforts to analyze such terms as 'good' and 'right' are the modern counterpart to the ancients' search for the essence of virtue and goodness. Thus, to say to a philosopher, "Define your terms. Tell me what you mean by 'good', and then we can begin to do ethics," or "It's all a matter of definition," is to misunderstand completely the nature of analytic philosophy. For the philosopher who can specify precisely what the meaning of 'good' is has already achieved some of the purposes with which one may set out to do ethics.

Yet it is not as if we do not know at all what 'good' means. If that were so, then we would have no basis for objecting when someone told us, for example, that 'good' means the same as 'weighs between 7 and 34 pounds'. We know that this is not what 'good' means, because, as speakers of English,

135

we have an intuitive understanding of the word. But that is not at all the same as being able to provide a precise and well-formulated definition of the term. Rather, we evaluate proposed definitions by comparing them with our intuitive understanding.

The dictionary, of course, provides definitions of all the terms that interest us. But dictionary definitions are not the kind that are of interest to philosophy, first, because dictionaries usually tell how words are used and, second, because dictionary definitions are circular. Let us now see how these two characteristics of dictionary definitions limit their usefulness in philosophy.

First, remember that we are seeking the meanings of terms. But telling how a word is used does not altogether give its meaning, because the use of a word is not the same as its meaning. Of course, in general, words could not be used the way they are if they didn't have the meanings they have, and they would not have the meanings they have if they were used differently. Use and meaning are thus closely related. But they are not quite the same. Consider the word 'angel'. We may *use* the word to describe an exceptional woman, but we don't intend to suggest that the woman literally *is* an angel. Rather, we are using the word metaphorically, in a way that depends on its literal meaning. We intend to suggest that the woman has certain angel-like qualities. It is just because the word 'angel' *means* what it does that we can use it in this way to describe something that is not really an angel.

The second limitation of dictionary definitions has to do with their circularity. Suppose, as an aesthetician, I am concerned to discover the nature of aesthetic value. I may begin by seeking the meaning of 'beautiful'. If I am told that 'x is beautiful' means 'x has beauty', I have been given a definition that surely everyone would agree is correct. But it is of no philosophical value, because it defines the word 'beautiful' in terms of the notion of beauty, and that is just what we set out to analyze. The definition has led us right back where we started: It is circular.

Some definitions are circular in a less obvious way. For example, someone may suggest as a definition of 'x is beautiful' the expression 'x enjoys the characteristic of positive aesthetic merit'. The circularity here is not as apparent as in the previous case. But a moment's reflection reveals that the expression we are interested in is defined in terms of a concept we do not understand, and, as if that alone were not enough to make the definition unsatisfactory, it was the attempt to understand that very concept that led us to seek the meaning of 'beautiful'. Thus here, too, we are led back to the place where we began; the circle is a bit larger, but it is nonetheless a circle. Even though they are ultimately circular, dictionary definitions are often helpful, because we usually understand the words used to define the term in question. But that dictionary definitions are always circular if followed far enough cannot be denied, because this circularity is guaranteed by the very attempt to define *each* word in the language in terms of other phrases in the language. Indeed, ultimate circularity can be avoided only by paying a price: The cost is that we must leave some words in the language undefined. Then the remaining words can be defined in terms of these *primitive* (i.e., undefined) expressions.

At this point, we should note that the word 'definition' is used ambiguously. That is, if we seek the meaning of A, and we are told that A means the same as B, we may speak of B as the definition of A. But we may also speak of the entire expression 'A means the same as B' as a definition. Since, in doing analytic philosophy, we wish to be as clear and precise as possible, we must find a way to eliminate the possibility of confusion arising from this ambiguity in the word 'definition'. We thus distinguish A and B as follows: We call the term that is defined the *definiendum*. In this case A is the definiendum. The term that gives the meaning of the definiendum—in this case, B—is called the *definiens*. We call the entire expression 'A means the same as B' a definition. Equivalently, we may say that A is equal to B *by definition*, which we abbreviate as: A = $_{df}$ B, writing the definiendum on the left and the definiens on the right.

It is a common opinion among people unfamiliar with analytic philosophy that the solution of philosophical problems is 'just a matter of definition'. They observe that any conclusion can be made to follow if one is permitted to define terms at will. For example, if I wish to show that causes must precede their effects in time, and I define 'cause' as 'an event that results in a later event', the conclusion I want is guaranteed by the definition. But the crucial point here is that one is *not* free to define terms at will. On the contrary, there are criteria that a definition must meet if it is to be philosophically acceptable. Thus merely finding a definition that will support the desired conclusion is not enough. The definition must also meet the criteria, and the criteria make tasks that are 'just a matter of definition' very difficult indeed.

We have already seen what some of the criteria for definition are. First, definitions must be in accord with intuitive understanding of the definiendum. This criterion is difficult to meet, in practice, because it requires that the definiens must preserve the many meaning connections that the definiendum has with other words in the language.

To illustrate: If we are trying to provide an adequate definition of 'motive', we must seek to insure that our definition does not entail that other closely connected words such as 'action' or 'desire' must be defined in ways that are contrary to our intuitive understanding of these latter terms. Or, to take a more detailed example, suppose we claim that the correct definition of 'evil' is (i) 'that which is contrary to God's law'. Although this definition may not obviously conflict with our intuitions about the meaning of 'evil', we must realize that it places certain constraints on what we can (consistently) mean by 'God', 'God's law', and 'contrary'.

It may be that our intuitive understanding of the word 'God' (for example, 'the omnipotent creator of the universe') is such that it is incompatible with definition (i)—because, for example, an omnipotent being does not ordain laws that can be broken. This line of reasoning raises questions about what we mean by 'omnipotent', and so on. In this way, the search for a philosophically adequate definition of a single expression almost always leads to a consideration of the meanings of many other related expressions.

In addition, philosophical definitions must not be circular, and the definiens must be expressed in language we can understand, or the definition is of no use. Besides, if we do not understand the definiens, there may be a hidden circularity in the definition. These criteria, in most philosophically interesting cases, are either very hard or impossible to meet. Consequently, the technique of *explication* has been developed as an alternative to definition.

The primary difference between explication and definition is that the criterion of accord with intuitive understanding is weakened in the former case. Outside of that, explication is much like definition. In fact, by analogy with definition, we introduce the technical terms *explicandum* and *explicatum* to refer respectively to the term we explicate and to the term or phrase we provide as a substitute for it. In seeking an explication for a term, we wish to capture as much of the meaning as we can characterize precisely. Thus, while we do insist on accord with intuitive understanding, we permit some deviation in the interest of gaining precision. For example, if we wish to explicate 'true', we might try as an explicatum the phrase 'in correspondence with the facts', even though this explicatum does not capture the meaning of 'true' as it is used in, say, 'a true Rembrandt' or 'a true woman'.

2. *Further Methods of Analysis*

Finding definitions or explications for philosophically important terms is not, of course, one of the primary goals of philosophy. It is, rather, a technique used in the pursuit of those goals. There are many other techniques that play a prominent part in philosophical analysis. Providing a *counterexample*, for instance, is a simple yet essential technique. A counterexample is merely an example which illustrates that a given general assertion is false. Consider the assertion that no United States President has ever been a Catholic. The fact that John F. Kennedy was both a Catholic and a United States President is a counterexample to that assertion. Or consider the assertion that no state is larger than Texas. The fact that Alaska is a state and is larger than Texas is the counterexample to that assertion. Similarly, if I assert that knowledge = $_{df}$ belief—that is, that 'belief' means the same as 'knowledge'—then the fact that one may be said to believe something, yet not to know it (if, for example, what he believes is false), provides a counterexample to my assertion that 'belief' means the same as 'knowledge'. We call such an illustration a counterexample to the definition.

Another important philosophical technique is that of *re-*

ductio ad absurdum. That is, we show a position to be unacceptable by showing that it leads to—or can be reduced to—something absurd or clearly unacceptable for some other reason. For example, consider the assertion that there is no reason for keeping a promise. We apply the technique as follows. We consider what 'There is no reason to keep a promise' means by considering what a promise is. A promise, by its very nature, is obligatory. If someone makes a promise, then he has an obligation to keep it. Of course, something may happen to override that obligation; that is, there may be strong reasons not to keep the promise. But there is always some reason to keep it, simply because, as a promise, it involves an obligation to do something, and being obliged to do something is a reason for doing it. The assertion we began with was that there is no reason for keeping a promise. But we have now seen that a promise is by its very nature something that there is a reason to keep. So the assertion comes down to saying there is no reason to do something that, by its very nature, there is a reason to do. Since this is absurd, the claim must be rejected—*if* our argument is valid *and* our assumptions about the nature of promises are acceptable.

Finally, let us consider a somewhat more detailed illustration of philosophical analysis. The concept of causation is a prominent subject of philosophical inquiry. Consider the assertion that the same cause can have many effects. If we wish to be in a position to judge whether or not this assertion is true, we must first become clear about what it means. But its meaning is really not clear at all in spite of the fact that it may at first glance appear to be a simple assertion. In fact, we can distinguish a number of different ways in which it may be taken; and it may turn out that whether it is true or false that the same cause can have many effects depends on which way we take it. This situation is a standard one in analytic philosophy, where we are often faced with the task of evaluating an assertion that is actually ambiguous.

If we wish to understand the assertion in question, we must first achieve some clarity about the terms used. If we have no understanding of the word 'cause', then we cannot understand an assertion about causes. The first thing we note is that the word 'cause' is itself used ambiguously. That is, we sometimes speak of a *particular* event as a cause, as when we say 'When you went out without a hat, that (your going out last night without a hat) caused your cold'. But sometimes we speak of a *kind* of event as a cause, as when we say 'Going out without a hat causes colds'. Here we are not speaking of any particular event but of the entire class of events of a certain kind—the class of events that can be described as instances of going out without a hat. Now we can distinguish particular events (for instance, *your* going out without a hat *last* night) from kinds of events (for instance, going out without a hat). We can give a name to a particular event—let us refer to your going out last night without a hat as 'p'. Thus, we can say that p caused your cold. Let us also give a name to the kind of event in question. We shall say that an event is an event of kind A if it is an instance of going out without a hat. Thus p is an event of kind A. There is just one p; it is a particular event. But there can be any number of events of kind A.

Now we are in a position to see the ambiguity in the claim 'The same cause can have many effects'. First, we see that the phrase 'the same cause' could refer to a *particular* event. An example might be p—your going out without a hat last night. One might then say that p can have many effects. But the phrase 'the same cause' may refer to causes

of the same kind. Thus, if I too go out without a hat and
I get a cough, one may say that the cause of my cough is
the same as the cause of your cold. That is *not* to say that
event p caused my cough. Rather, it is to say that my cough
and your cold were both caused by events of the same kind,
kind A.

We shall now distinguish two senses of the assertion in
question. 'The same cause can have many effects' may mean:

(1) Two or more different events of the same type
    (for example, A) can have effects of different types
    (for example, coughs or colds).
(2) One event (for example, p) can have many effects.

But (2) is itself ambiguous, because the phrase 'many effects'
is in need of analysis. For example, if we say that p can have
many effects, we may mean that the event p can result in a
reprimand from your wife when you return, *and* a cold
tomorrow, *and* loss of hair later. We are saying that one
event (such as p) can have many subsequent effects (say, a,
b, and c). On the other hand, we may mean that there
are several different possible events any one of which could
result from p, depending on the circumstances. For example,
p could result in your getting a cold if it rains, *or* your
winning a bet (for example, that if you leave your hat at home
it will not rain) if it doesn't. Thus, we are saying that
one event (for example, p) could result in one of many effects
(b or d or e), depending on what happens. Thus (2) may mean:

(2a) One event (such as p) can have many subsequent
     effects, or
(2b) One event (such as p) could have various outcomes,
     depending on the circumstances.

We shall not carry the analysis any further, nor shall we be concerned with evaluating assertions (1), (2a), and (2b). Rather, we intend the analysis carried out so far to provide an illustration of actual philosophical activity and an example of the care with which such activity must be performed.

Exercises

1. Give an example of a plausible definition; identify the *definiendum* and *definiens*.

2. What are three criteria of adequacy for definition? Give examples of purported definitions each of which fails to meet one or more of the criteria you have cited.

*3. Show by counterexample that some claim is false.

4. Explain the argumentative technique of *reductio ad absurdum*.

VIII

Reading and Writing Philosophy

1. Reading Philosophy

The fact that philosophical writing is typically discursive, and sometimes of great literary merit, must not mislead one into thinking that philosophy books can be digested rapidly or understood on first reading. Indeed, the student is well advised to approach a philosophy book much as one would approach a physics text or an essay in mathematics.

It is impossible, of course, to lay down a set of rules about how one must read philosophy. Every person should develop his or her own method of reading and understanding written material. Therefore, the following remarks should be regarded as a suggested approach to the reading of philosophy, setting forth what will generally be found to be the minimum requirements for understanding a piece of philosophical discourse.

A. Read the work through to the end, *sympathetically*, in order to become familiar with the organization of the work, the author's style, and the major problems to which the selection, article, or book is addressed.

B. Reread the work more carefully; try to isolate the issues and arguments.

C. Read the work in detail, proceeding slowly and analyzing each argument as it arises. One may want to outline certain passages or translate particular arguments into the notation of symbolic logic in order to clarify their structure.

D. Reread the work *in toto* to grasp the overall aims and conclusions of the author and to evaluate the consistency of the argument. It is only at this point, after each component argument has been mastered, that the work can be completely understood.

When reading philosophy, keep in mind that the author is typically trying to establish some conclusion rather than to report some facts. To read sympathetically is to try to understand the author's project in ways which make it most likely to be a reasonable undertaking. To read sympathetically is not necessarily to agree with the author's conclusion. In fact if one disagrees with the position taken by a philosopher, it is all the more important to construe it sympathetically, to exercise what is sometimes called "The Principle of Maximum Charity." For if one is criticizing an argument, regardless of where one finds it, the criticism is most effective if it tells against the most favorable interpretation of the argument. Conversely, if one agrees with the conclusion of an argument and finds it to be well supported by the premises, it is all the more important to examine it with critical scrutiny in order to try to offer additional support at its weakest points.

Previewing the next section of this chapter, we may draw a lesson about writing philosophy papers from this discussion. Assuming that one agrees with one's own conclusions and with one's own arguments, we call attention to the particular need to read one's own work *unsympathetically*! Because one often thinks of more support for a position than he or she in fact writes, it is a good idea to put away a paper one has written and reread it a few days later, keeping a sharp eye out for gaps in the arguments that are presented to the reader. For even if those gaps were absent in the thoughts of the writer, what is actually written is the reader's only access to the argument.

Philosophy, like most technical writing, must be read *actively*. One must carry on a silent dialogue with the author, questioning assertions at every turn and accepting conclusions only after they have been carefully tested. The following are some questions that should be kept in mind while reading, particularly when one is analyzing the arguments in detail (step C, above).

What problem is the author trying to solve? Does the formulation of the problem rest on any assumptions, tacit or explicitly stated?

How is he or she treating the problem? What is his or her method of solution?

On what assumptions are the author's arguments based?

What assumptions are needed for the argument, even though not explicitly stated?

Is the argument valid? Is it sound?

How does each particular argument fit into the work as a whole? Is it necessary to the main argument?

If the author has made a mistake, is it an instructive one? How is it that the author was led astray? Perhaps in formulating an answer to this last question, one will hit upon a general mistake, which is likely to be made in other contexts as well.

2. *Writing Philosophy*

Analytic philosophy is an activity that is pursued in the hope of achieving precision and clarity about the concepts, logical structure, methods, and objects of human knowledge. Thus precision and clarity are minimal criteria of acceptability in philosophical writing. But precision and clarity, sad to say, are as hard to achieve as excellence in style. Whoever wishes to do philosophical analysis, therefore, must consciously endeavor to meet the standards that the discipline imposes.

As with other kinds of writing, the only way to learn to write philosophy is by making the attempt. One must write, subject the result to careful criticism, and then write again, bearing in mind the criticism. But it is not only others who can provide such beneficial criticism. On the contrary, the ability to read one's own writing with critical scrutiny is a major asset to writers of all sorts and a mark of successful writers in any field. Yet one can be usefully critical, of oneself or of others, only to the extent to which one has standards of criticism.

Everything that has been said above about reading philosophy is equally true when it is one's own philosophical writing that is being read. Thus remarks about what to look for when reading philosophy provide some basis for self-criticism in writing philosophy. If one knows what to look for in the writing of others, then one can, insofar as it is possible to remain objective, evaluate one's own work. But the tendency is to read one's own writing with extraordinary sympathy—to overlook failings that would be immediately apparent in the writing of others. Thus reading one's own philosophy critically is generally more difficult than reading the work of others.

Some progress in the effort to be objectively self-critical may result from explicit consideration of the nature of common failings in philosophical writing. Such consideration should, at least, alert the beginning writer of philosophy to specific dangers to which one is likely to fall victim. We shall therefore present in the remainder of this section a discussion of some characteristic weaknesses of beginning papers in philosophy. The material in the following two sections should be of some use in helping the writer to avoid those weaknesses.

A student's first writing in philosophy is commonly very unclear. This lack of clarity results from many factors, some of which can be explicitly isolated. Among the most common are:

A. The use of phrases and expressions that have no meaning, or no meaning that is clear in the context. Consider in this connection the phrase 'the *nearly infinite* value of a human life'. What does 'nearly infinite' mean—large but finite? Or actually infinite?

B. The use of equivocal (that is, ambiguous) terms or phrases as if they were univocal. Consider: 'The *purpose* of this knife is to cut grapefruit'. Does 'purpose' in this sentence mean the purpose for which the knife was designed or the purpose for which it is used? It may be a knife designed specifically to cut grapefruit or it may be a bent steak knife that is used to cut grapefruit.

C. Reliance on unexplained metaphors or analogies. For example, 'The human mind is like a computer'. In what specific ways is it like a computer? Certainly not in being made of metal.

D. Reliance on jargon—that is, the use of phrases which have a familiar or authoritative ring but little content. Consider: 'Without absolute standards there can be no moral worth'. The phrase 'absolute standard' is a familiar one, but it is used in so many different ways that its meaning in this context is not clear.

More generally, papers in philosophy commonly suffer from a lack of substantial content. This lack is often due in part to one or more of the following mistakes:

A. Failure to take note of important relevant distinctions, such as failure to distinguish, in a paper about values, between what *is* and what *ought to be*.

B. Overemphasis on a single aspect of a problem—for example, in a discussion of principles of education, speaking of people as economic or intellectual beings without mentioning or justifying the restriction to these aspects of people.

C. Failure to formulate the problem at hand in a precise and clear way.

D. Failure to come to grips with a problem once it is formulated. This failing frequently results in papers which, while not containing assertions or arguments that are themselves objectionable, provide more wind than substance. Usually, assertions in papers of this type, if they are intelligible, are so vague and general that it is difficult to imagine how they could be doubted or why they need be said.

E. Failure to perceive the lack of precision in ordinary language. Just what, for example, does it mean to say, as people often do, that morality is objective? Is it objective because it is measurable by scientific observation, as the weight of a stone is, or what?

F. Failure to reread critically to insure both that one has said what he or she has meant to say and that one means what he or she has in fact said.

3. Use and Mention

In this section, as throughout this book, we have occasion to talk *about* words, to *mention* a word rather than to *use* it. The device of using single quotation marks to indicate that a word is being mentioned and not used is found frequently in philosophical writings and is deserving of attention here.

An author writing about Franklin Delano Roosevelt will have many occasions to mention the thirty-second President. One might mention Roosevelt, for example, in any sentence that is about Roosevelt and mention the thirty-second President by using his name or some description that uniquely describes Roosevelt. In the preceding two sentences, Roosevelt has been mentioned six times, four times by using his name and twice by using a definite description: 'the thirty-second President'. A man and his name are quite different entities; one is an animal, the other an element of language. Sentences are composed of elements of a language; one could not use Roosevelt himself in a sentence any more than one could shake hands with Roosevelt's name.

Analogously, when one talks about a word or mentions a word in a sentence, one does so by using the name of that word in the sentence. But the name of a word is also a word; both are elements of language, both can be used in sentences, and thus they may easily be confused. The name of a word is formed by enclosing the word within *single* quotation marks. A name formed in this way refers to the *word* of which it is a name, just as Roosevelt's name refers to the man of whom it is a name. The name of a word does not refer to the object or objects referred to by the word of which it is a name. A word may not refer to any object, but its name always refers to the word. For example, 'is' does not refer to any object, but ''is'' refers to a word. Let us consider some further examples:

(1) Red is a color.
(2) 'Red' is a three-letter word.
(3) John is a boy.
(4) 'John' is a boy's name.

Each of these sentences is true, whereas the following sentences are false:

(5) Red is a three-letter word.
(6) 'Red' is a color.
(7) 'John' is a boy.
(8) John is a boy's name.

Sentence (5) is false because it states that a color is a word, while (6) is false because it states that a word is a color. Sentences (7) and (8) reveal a similar confusion of a name with the name of a name. Sometimes we may wish to refer to a word in a sentence; consider these examples:

(9) 'Red' in sentence (5) refers to a color.
(10) "Red" in sentence (6) refers to a word.
(11) "Red" appears in sentence (6), but 'red' does not.

Each of these sentences is true, but the following sentence is false because it states that a word which refers to a color refers to a word:

(12) 'Red' in sentence (5) refers to a word.

We may form the name of a sentence, a predicate, or a description in an analogous way. Consider:

(13) 'John believes it hailed yesterday' is an intentional sentence.
(14) 'is a Senator from California' is a predicate true of Senator Cranston.
(15) 'The Senator from California' fails to describe one and only one individual.

Notice that the following sentence is not even grammatically correct, because there is no subject of the verb 'is':

(16) John believes it hailed yesterday is an intensional sentence.

In sentence (10) we used the name of a name of a word. We form the name of a name just as we form the name of any other word, by enclosing the name in single quotation marks. Similarly we can form the name of a name of a name, etc., the limit to this procedure being one of intelligibility rather than one of logic.

4. Words to Watch

Words are used for various purposes. Some words that suffice for use in everyday communication do not suffice for philosophical discussions, perhaps because they are vague in their ordinary use. Or perhaps it is because it has been to the philosopher's interest to draw fine distinctions with which one is not concerned outside of philosophical study and that therefore are not reflected in words as they are ordinarily used. Below we shall mention some words and phrases that are best avoided in philosophical discussions and some that should be used only with considered caution.

Semantics is most commonly understood by philosophers as theory of meaning, encompassing questions about the sense and reference of words. As such, it is concerned with the relations between a sign (or word) and what the sign signifies (or means). Semantics in this sense may be contrasted with syntactics, which is concerned in part with formal relations between signs and with the rules by which signs may be combined to yield well-formed formulas (sentences) in a given language. (See the section on syntax, semantics, and pragmatics in Chapter III.) There are indeed many *semantical questions*, including those problems concerning sentences, words, and meaning mentioned in Chapters IV and V, as well as questions in the theory of truth and questions concerning the relations between a name and the object it names.

But to say that something is "just a matter of semantics" or "just a question of semantics" can be misleading. We have seen in the previous discussion of philosophical analysis that definitions in accord with strict criteria may be a goal of some philosophical investigation. But to suppose that one can dismiss a philosophical problem by asserting that it is just a matter of definition or semantics is to miss the point of what a philosophical problem is, if such an assertion is intended to imply that the problem can be solved by arbitrarily defining certain terms. Arbitrary definitions will not solve any philosophical problem.

Whether it is sentences or propositions that can be true, a particular sentence or proposition is either true or false. To say that a sentence is *really true* is to say no more than that it is true. And to say that one sentence is *more true* or *closer to the truth* than another is often to engender confusion. If two sentences are both true, they are equally true. If both are false, then neither is true, nor is one more true than the other. If one sentence is true and another false, it may be appropriate to speak of the first as more true than the second, but this locution does not convey any more information about the sentences than is conveyed simply by saying that one is true and the other false. It may, of course, be that there is better evidence for one sentence than another or better reason to believe one than another. Instead of saying of such sentences that one is more true than the other, it is clearer to show that the evidence for the one is better than that for the other.

The words '*subjective*', '*objective*', '*relative*', and '*absolute*' have often been used by philosophers. But no one of these terms has had only one use. It is safe to say that these words should be avoided as much as possible. Whenever something is said to be relative, one must also say to *what* it is relative. "What is right is relative" is not a complete assertion until one has said whether what is right is relative to a particular society, individual, or what; and how. When 'absolute' is used with the intention of conveying the idea 'not relative', the question "Not relative to what?" becomes relevant. Like 'relative' and 'absolute', the words 'subjective' and 'objective' have often been assumed to be opposite in meaning. But since none of these four words has either a clear meaning or a standardized use in philosophical discussions, this opposition is of no help in clarifying the meaning of any of these words. It is worth noting that 'subjective' need not be a pejorative adjective, nor 'objective' an adjective of commendation. Each of these words should be used only with an explanation of how and why it is being used. Often such an explanation suffices to make the point for which the word seemed useful.

The words discussed below are used clearly only when certain questions are answered about each particular use. Consider the assertion that two events or objects are *similar*, *alike*, or *different*. Such assertions are interesting only when it is said in what respects the things are similar or different, because no matter how different any two things are, there is some respect in which they are alike; and no matter how similar or alike two things are, they are different in some respect. For example, two sentences may be alike in being extensional but different in their truth value; two objects may be without perceptible difference in color, size, and shape, and yet be in different places. Referring back to section 1 of Chapter III, you will see that analogous remarks are applicable to the word 'same'. We often say of one object that it is different from what it once was, that it has *changed* or is *changing*. Just as one needs to specify in what ways two different things are different, so must one say in what respects one and the same thing has changed or is different. The assertion that two objects or events are the same and yet different need not be contradictory, although it may be. Its meaning simply is not clear until it is indicated in what respect, or in relation to which properties, the objects are the same and different.

The words '*efficient*', '*deficient*', '*perfect*', '*complete*', and '*adequate*' similarly call for an answer to the questions "In what respects?" or "By what standards?" or "For what purposes?" Thus a knife may be efficient for cutting meat and inefficient for turning screws. A rose may be a perfect flower but an imperfect source of nourishment. A student's program of study may be adequate for a high school diploma but inadequate for college admission. And a cereal may be complete as a supply of vitamin requirements for a child but incomplete for an adolescent.

The words '*object*', '*entity*', '*event*', and '*thing*' must be used with one caution in mind. None of these words provides a criterion for individuation; that is, one can know the meaning of the word 'thing' and still be unable to distinguish one thing from another. In contrast, anyone who knows the meaning of the word 'man' can distinguish one man from another or count the number of men in a room. But suppose that one were asked to count the number of things or objects in a room in which there were ten men. One would not know whether to count each leg as an entity or whether to count arms as well as hands as things. Thus to say of anything that it is an entity or an object or a thing is to provide little or no information about it.

Words or sentences that have no clearly defined meaning or use may be said to be *vague*. The word 'absolute' is vague, as is the sentence 'There are no absolute standards of morality'. In contrast, an *ambiguous* word or sentence is one that has more than one meaning. 'Bridge' is an ambiguous word, and if Jones is a man who builds spans over water and wears false teeth, the sentence 'Jones's new bridge is poorly designed' is ambiguous.

It is also said that a word or sentence is *meaningless*. Some philosophers have asserted that the sentence 'God exists' is meaningless because it is neither analytic nor confirmable by experience. Clearly such an assertion presupposes a standard of meaningfulness—namely, that any statement which is meaningful is either analytic or subject to empirical confirmation. So when a word or sentence is asserted to be meaningless, the question "By what criterion of meaningfulness?" is in order. Most frequently, the assertion that a sentence is meaningless is intended to indicate that the sentence has no content and conveys no information. Therefore, a meaningless sentence is neither true nor false; that is, it has no content on the basis of which its truth value could be determined.

Exercises

1. Illustrate the difference between use and mention.

*2. Indicate the truth value of the following:

    (a) Blue has four letters.
    (b) 'Red' is a color.
    (c) John is a boy's name.
    (d) 'Red' has four letters.
    (e) Blue is a color.

3. Distinguish between vagueness and ambiguity.

4. What is wrong with the question 'How many things are there in this room?'

*5. What is suspect about the following claim? 'Since men and apes are so much alike and porpoises are so unlike both, apes will exhibit a high degree of problem-solving ability whereas porpoises will not'.

IX

Divisions of Philosophy

1. Introduction

Philosophy is a broad field of study within which it is possible to delimit more specific areas of inquiry. Such divisions have been made traditionally on the basis of the nature of the questions considered in each area. In this chapter, we shall deal with the general content of the major areas of philosophy by indicating some problems illustrative of each area. But these problems we mention will hardly be exhaustive of the areas; rather, they are selected as typical. Moreover, it is a serious error to suppose that a question in philosophy falls neatly within one specialized area. In fact, there are many problems in philosophy that are of major concern to specialists in several areas. In such cases, one can think of the areas in philosophy as representing not so much various sets of questions but rather various points of view from which the questions are to be considered. Thus it is rare indeed that real progress in one area of philosophy does not shed some light in other areas. And as one might expect, a mark of the importance of a problem in philosophy is the extent to which it permeates the various divisions within the field.

The picture we will provide of the divisions of philosophy will thus be rough—but that is well, for the divisions are rough; and it would be a great mistake to consider them to be clearly delineated.

2. *Theory of Value*

ETHICS

We evaluate our own and others' actions; for example:

> (1) Dr. Smith will do the *right* thing if she tells her patient the truth about his illness.
> (2) I am *obligated* to repay the money I borrowed from Bill.

Evaluations can also be made of kinds of actions; for example:

> (3) It is always *right* to tell the truth.
> (4) Repaying debts is *obligatory*.

And evaluations can be made of people as agents—that is, persons who act; for example:

> (5) Smith did not have to accept the offer; she was *free* to do as she chose.
> (6) Jones was *worthy of praise* for saving Brown from drowning.

Speaking generally, we may say that each of these examples is an assertion about moral value. Ethics is, in part, an investigation into the nature of moral judgment and moral reasoning. Typical of the questions that fall within the scope of ethics is the following: If a man says that an act is right, is he just saying something about himself—for example, that he approves of the act; or is he saying something about the property rightness, which the act has independently of his attitude? Closely linked with this question is the question of what facts about the act one could cite as evidence for the correctness of judgments of the kinds exemplified above by (1) to (6). If such a judgment is only a report of the feelings of the judge toward the act, is any evidence about the act relevant to determining the truth value of the judgment?

Questions in ethics then are not specific questions about whether a particular act is right or wrong; ethics is to be distinguished from moralizing or casuistry. Ethical arguments are not exhortations to some course of action. It is true that philosophers writing in ethics have not always avoided giving moral advice. But ethical philosophers, *qua* philosophers, discuss instead the *nature of reasoning* about moral matters and propose criteria on the basis of which such reasoning is to be evaluated.

What distinguishes good from bad reasons offered in favor of moral judgments? One sometimes supports a particular judgment [for example, (1) above] by appeal to a general principle [for example, (3) above]. But philosophers have been concerned to determine in just what way general principles do support particular claims. Imagine a disagreement between Mrs. Black and Mr. White. Black argues that (1) is a correct judgment because the doctor's telling her patient the truth is a particular instance of the kind of action mentioned in (3). White denies that (1) is correct; he cites another general principle, that a doctor is obliged to do whatever is possible to improve the patient's condition. White asserts that this patient's condition would be worsened by his knowledge of the severity of his condition and therefore that for Dr. Smith to tell the patient the truth must be wrong because to do so is to violate the doctor's obligation to improve her patient's health.

This supposed disagreement raises several problems that have concerned ethical philosophers. First we see that the general principles to which White and Black appeal support conflicting judgments about the moral value of a particular act. Perhaps we must evaluate the general principles before we can judge the cogency of the arguments presented. One may ask whether there can be evidence for general principles at all; perhaps we should evaluate a principle by inquiring into the acceptability of the particular judgments it supports. But if we argue that general principles support particular judgments and that acceptability of a general principle is to be decided on the basis of the judgments it supports, our argument seems to be circular.

In this dispute, White cited a fact about the patient's condition, the fact that the patient's condition would deteriorate if he learned of the severity of his illness. Philosophers have often discussed the role that facts such as this, which do not themselves involve value judgments, play in moral reasoning. Is it always possible to distinguish descriptive or factual claims from evaluative claims? How can factual evidence ever be relevant to moral judgments?

It has often been argued that unless one understands the meaning of such terms as 'right', 'obligatory', 'free', and 'responsible', which are used in ethical judgments, one cannot begin to answer other questions in ethics. Thus some writers in ethics have attempted to define or explicate 'right' or the rightness of an action either in terms of its consequences or in terms of the motives from which it was done.

Other writers have argued that no noncircular definition is possible. Still others have argued that such terms as 'right' have no meaning but rather are used simply to express approval.

Inquiry into the meaning of expressions used in ethical judgments is relevant to the question of what is evidence for a moral judgment. If we believe that 'right' means 'done from altruistic motives', then whatever is evidence that an act was done from altruistic motives is at the same time evidence that the act was right. The question of evidence is central to the problem of evaluating a person's moral reasoning or of adjudicating between the disputants in an argument concerning matters of value.

Discussion of the rightness or wrongness of actions has been closely connected with discussions of the moral worth of agents. Philosophers have been concerned to discuss what reasons are relevant to the evaluation of a person as, for example, praiseworthy or blameworthy for an action. Problems concerning the logical relations between a person's being free and being responsible and between his or her being responsible and being worthy of praise or blame have been considered throughout the history of ethical philosophy.

AESTHETICS

Not all evaluations are of actions; not all value is ethical value. We judge one painting to be better than another, evaluate the rhythm of a poem, criticize the form of a sculpture. One studies such evaluations in aesthetics, but judgments about beauty are not limited to works of art. They may apply as well to natural objects and events, such as mountains and sunsets. Thus, aesthetics is not limited to the study of evaluations of artifacts. In fact, one of the questions that interest aestheticians is whether or not there is any way to delimit the range of objects that can have aesthetic value.

Analogously to questioning in ethics, one may ask whether or not the beauty of an object can be defined in terms of some or all of the object's descriptive properties or qualities. Does the subject matter of a work of art contribute to its aesthetic value? For example, if kindness is better than cruelty, is a poem praising kindness better than one praising cruelty?

The question also arises whether there can be any basis for criticizing someone's judgment that a painting or poem is beautiful. Is such a judgment merely an expression of taste? Or do aesthetic judgments, like those in science, stand in need of justification? If so, how can they be defended?

Aesthetics is not art criticism; aestheticians are not concerned to evaluate particular works of art or to advise artists how to create better works of art. Rather, aestheticians have typically been concerned with such questions as whether there is an aesthetic attitude, a particular way in which one must regard an object, in order to appreciate its aesthetic value or beauty. Writers in aesthetics have proposed and criticized criteria for the evaluation of aesthetic judgments; they have proposed and criticized general principles that might support particular judgments; finally, they have often discussed whether any such criteria are even possible.

GENERAL VALUE THEORY

Some philosophers have argued that we would better understand both ethical and aesthetic judgments if we could view such judgments in the wider context of evaluation in general. Besides evaluating human animals and their actions and works of art, we also evaluate such diverse things as tools, food, athletes, mechanical skills, amusements, and techniques. And we engage in such different—but related— activities as grading, appreciating, praising, recommending, instituting, legislating, and criticizing. Many of these objects of evaluation and ways of evaluating are significantly different from the topics traditionally treated under the heading of ethics or aesthetics.

Indeed, it may be the case that by concentrating on the moral and the beautiful we have distorted both the importance and the peculiar role of aesthetic and ethical judgments and have failed to notice important similarities between, for example, good people and good typewriters or between morally good actions and skillful performances. But, be that as it may, these other modes of evaluation are philosophically important and interesting in their own right if for no other reason than that they make up the bulk of our day-to-day evaluative judgments.

3. *Epistemology*

There are many things that we claim to know—for example: (1) that all men are animals, (2) that Lassie is a collie, (3) that cigarette smoking is causally related to lung cancer, and (4) that every event has a cause. We are not usually called upon to justify our claims to knowledge. But if a man who lives across the street were to assert that there are green men living on Mars, we might well ask how he knew or what his evidence was. If he replied that he knew because he had seen green Martians in his crystal ball, we would question both the acceptability of his evidence and the truth of his original assertion.

Epistemology is an inquiry into the nature of knowledge. But the epistemologist is not asking what the evidence is for *particular* knowledge claims. Rather, part of the inquiry of epistemology is directed toward ascertaining what *kind* of evidence is relevant to a particular *kind* of knowledge claim. For example, the statement that no crystal ball vision is evidence relevant to an empirical claim is an epistemological assertion. It was the observation that there are different kinds of claims to knowledge, requiring different sorts of evidence, that led philosophers to draw the distinctions discussed in Chapter VI between analytic and synthetic sentences and between *a priori* and *a posteriori* knowledge.

In the course of investigating the relation between the evidence for an assertion and the assertion itself, the epistemologist may ask whether the evidence must be known with certainty. For example, does the fact that we may sometimes be misled by our senses invalidate perception as a source of evidence? Since the evidence for some claims [such as (2) above] must be at least in part perceptual, one who argues that perception is not a reliable source of evidence thereby argues that no empirical statement like (2) can ever be known to be true. And, in so arguing, one would be offering a partial answer to an epistemological question— what sorts of things can we know?

We have suggested that the task of the epistemologist differs from that of the scientist. Consider, as illustrative of the point, the question of how or whether we are able to see colors. The physicist or physiologist may take this question to be equivalent to the question of how we make color discriminations. He or she may then study physical conditions of sight such as illumination, eye structure, and neurological connections between the eye and the brain. The philosopher, on the other hand, may argue that we do not see colors at all. What we see, the philosopher may claim, are colored objects. If A sees X, then X appears some way to A. But colors don't appear any way to anyone. Objects can appear red, but how does red appear? Does it ever look orange? Objects can appear different than they are, but how can colors do this? Thus the philosopher's approach includes conceptual analysis of what it means to say that someone sees something.

Another problem typical of epistemological inquiry concerns the status of induction as a source of evidence for claims to knowledge.

Inductive arguments begin with particular observation statements or a statement summarizing particular observations; they have as conclusions either (1) a general statement, not all of whose particular instances are known, or (2) a particular statement about an as yet unknown state of affairs. An example of (1) is:

> All presidents of the United States thus far have been men.
> (Therefore) All presidents of the United States will be men.

And an example of (2) is:

> All presidents of the United States thus far have been men.
> (Therefore) The next president of the United States will be a man.

Neither of these arguments is deductively valid; it is logically possible that the next president of the United States will be a woman, even though the above premise is true.

Although logicians have criteria for the admissibility of rules of deductive inference as well as a complete and sound set of rules that satisfy these criteria, no such criteria or set of rules exist for inductive arguments. And because it is always logically possible that the conclusion of an inductive argument may be false even though its premises are true, some philosophers have argued that induction does not provide an acceptable source of evidence, that the mere fact that some proposition is the conclusion of an inductive argument cannot constitute sufficient reason for a claim to know that that proposition is true. The philosophical discussion of induction resembles the discussion of the status of perceptual evidence in that it is a general inquiry into what, if anything, constitutes good evidence for a particular type of claim.

Argument by analogy is sometimes considered a type of inductive argument. Attention has been directed toward the question of the validity of this kind of argument because it has seemed a method by which we might justify claims of knowledge about others' minds—for example, about what another person believes. We cannot observe another's mind, but we can observe his or her actions. Suppose Ms. Smith is acting exactly as I do when I believe that it is going to rain today. When I act as she is now acting, I do so because I believe it will rain today. I can observe these likenesses in behavior and then conclude that we are alike in beliefs as well—that is, that she believes it is going to rain today. Yet there is always the logical possibility that she acts as she does because she holds a belief different from mine—for example, that taking an umbrella will prevent rain. In an argument by analogy, it is observed that certain of the properties of some things are the same, in this case that Smith is acting as I act when I believe it will rain. On the basis of the observed similarities, it is concluded that the things are also alike in some unobserved respects, in this case that we are alike in our belief that it will rain.

Not all epistemological questions are directly concerned with the relation between evidence and a proposition that someone claims to know. We claim to know not only propositions but persons, objects, and places. Knowledge of the former kind is typically expressed by means of the 'knows that' construction, knowledge of the latter sort by means of the grammatical direct object construction; for instance, knowing Senator Cranston or knowing San Francisco.

Bertrand Russell made a distinction between two types of knowledge which parallels the one we have just indicated, and he used it in his philosophy. He called propositional knowledge, knowledge by description; and he called direct object knowledge, knowledge by acquaintance. He already raised the important question: How are these two kinds of knowledge related to each other? In some other languages they are expressed by different verbs. Do they really have something in common? Is one of them perhaps reducible to the other, as Russell claimed that knowledge by description can be reconstructed in terms of knowledge by acquaintance?

There is also the kind of knowledge expressed by the construction 'knows' + a *wh*-word; for instance, knows who, knows what, knows where, knows why. Many interesting and challenging kinds of knowledge are expressed by these constructions (as well as by our claims to know *how* to perform many activities and to accomplish many tasks). How is the knowledge expressed by these *wh*-constructions related to the other two kinds of knowledge? Clearly, knowing who someone is does not imply knowing him or her, nor does knowing a person imply that one knows who he or she is. But are there perhaps subtler connections between the two constructions? What logical form or forms do the different kinds of knowledge claims have? The same distinctions as we have made for knowledge can be made for several other concepts which are important in epistemology, including those expressed by 'remembers', 'perceives', and 'sees', and the same questions can be asked about them as were asked concerning knowledge. Will the answers be the same for all the different concepts? What is common to all the different analogous constructions—for instance, common to all the *wh*-constructions? Do they have the same logical form? Why do other epistemologically interesting verbs fail to have all the three types of constructions? (For instance, there is no *wh* construction with 'believes', nor is there any direct object construction whose meaning would be parallel to 'knows' + a direct object. Why?) What are the relations of the other epistemic concepts to knowledge? Are these relationships logical or factual? Can we characterize memory in terms of knowledge, or perhaps knowledge in terms of perception and memory? It is clear that these questions have to be answered before any philosopher can claim to possess a fully satisfactory theory of knowledge.

A partly overlapping group of problems concerns the definition of knowledge and its recognizability. Plato already considered the suggestion that knowledge could be equated with true belief, but rejected the suggestion. What more can we require of knowledge? It has been proposed that in order for a person, P, to know that S, it does not suffice that S is in fact the case and that P believes it; in addition, P must be *justified* in believing that S. This definition of knowledge has several variants, depending on what one takes the relevant kinds of justification to be. Recently, sharp criticism has been leveled both at the general idea of such a definition of knowledge as justified true belief and at some of its more particularized variants. One variant interprets 'being justified in believing that S' as possessing evidence that makes S more probable than some constant probability level $1 - \varepsilon$. The prospects of this definition have been the subject of a lively discussion in the recent literature. It cannot be upheld in its unqualified form, as is shown by various counterexamples, the best known of which is referred to as the "*Lottery Paradox.*"

When one knows something, must one be aware that one knows? This question has often been formulated by asking: When one knows, does one always know that one knows? However, it turns out that the phrase 'knowing that one knows' has several other uses, too. Their interrelations and their relation to the justification of knowledge claims present interesting further problems to epistemologists and have frequently been discussed by them.

4. *Metaphysics*

We have said that many questions are studied from the standpoint of one or another specialized area of philosophy and that it is impossible to give more than a rough delineation of the divisions within philosophy. Nowhere is it more difficult to isolate an area by reference to its problems than in metaphysics. One reason for this difficulty is that throughout the history of philosophy many problems have at one time been called metaphysical and at other times been denied that appellation. Some philosophers, distressed by the sort of speculation that has been called metaphysics, have denied that the problems with which they were concerned were metaphysical ones. Others have argued that these philosophers were nevertheless still dealing with traditional problems of metaphysics and that no renaming of a problem would change its nature. With these difficulties in mind, let us make some general remarks about some problems that have most usually been called metaphysical and about the status of the propositions of metaphysics.

Metaphysics is concerned with the way in which we think about the world. Some metaphysicians have held that the concepts basic to our thought could not be other than they are. They have gone on to inquire into which concepts must be presupposed by the structure of our thought. We distinguish individuals—the sorts of things that possess properties—from the properties they possess. This distinction, often referred to as between particulars and universals, has been cited as an example of a distinction fundamental to our way of thinking; and it has brought forth many questions in metaphysics. For example, what are the criteria by which we individuate particulars—in other words, distinguish one particular object from another? On what grounds do we say that the butterfly that emerges from a cocoon is one and the same animal as the caterpillar that spun the cocoon? Do the criteria for individuating people imply that there are some essential properties that an object must possess in order to be a person? Suppose, for example, that a person loses all reasoning power; is what remains still a person? Or are there some changes a person could undergo, after which what remains would no longer be a person?

Regarding universals, it has been long debated whether or not they exist independently of their being manifested in particulars. Could there, for example, be whiteness if there were no white objects? Further, one may ask how universals can be individuated one from another. Can one explain the difference between redness and greenness with no reference to red or green particulars?

Not all metaphysicians have accepted the way in which we normally think about the world as inevitable or even correct. Some have suggested that we alter the structure of our thought, arguing, for example, that the world we perceive through our senses is but an appearance of some transcendent reality. Many have gone on to consider the nature of this supposed reality, suggesting that it consists of some sort of mind or collection of ideas, rather than of physical matter.

Such questions, about just what it is that actually exists, are called *ontological* questions. Thus the question of whether universals exist independently of the particulars that instantiate them is an ontological question. Some philosophers have argued that universals do exist but in a different sense of the word 'exist' from that in which particulars are said to exist. Whether the word 'exist' is genuinely equivocal in such a way is open to question.

The question of just what kinds of things exist is one of importance to many areas of philosophy, and thus philosophers have studied in detail the consequences of various answers. If matter is held to be the only kind of thing that exists and if, in addition, matter is subject to causal laws, can there be freedom of the will? The answer to this question is of importance, for example, in moral and legal philosophy, where questions of responsibility arise. On the other hand, if one is an idealist—that is, if one holds that ideas alone exist—various epistemological questions arise at once. For instance, how can sensory experience be evidence for a proposition about ideas?

It is often difficult to know what would count as evidence for a metaphysical claim. The proposition that universals exist independently of particulars would usually be regarded as synthetic. Yet it seems totally unsusceptible of an *a posteriori* proof. In general, metaphysical claims are synthetic but admit only of an *a priori* proof. As you have read in Chapter VI, many philosophers deny that there can be any *a priori* proof of a synthetic statement. Therefore, they question whether metaphysical statements can ever be known to be true. In discussions of the status of metaphysical propositions and the knowledge we can have of them, the distinction between metaphysics and epistemology is difficult, if not impossible, to draw. Similarly, questions of freedom and determinism bring ethics and metaphysics together; and there is a close connection between logic and metaphysics. For in the discussion of the predicate calculus, it was pointed out that the logician must specify the range of the variables, the types of entities for which the variables stand. But what types of entities there are, what types of things the variables can stand for, is surely a metaphysical question.

Finally, metaphysics is often inseparable from the philosophy of language. Some metaphysicians have claimed that the syntactic and semantic structure of our language blinds us to certain features of reality while overemphasizing other features, and they have recommended linguistic changes designed to meet these difficulties. Others have claimed that such wholesale changes lead to incoherence.

5. Logic

Logic is a philosophical study of certain properties of human reasoning. A psychologist might be interested in how people reason; common forms of incorrect reasoning would be as interesting to her or him as common forms of correct reasoning. But the logician's concern is with an analysis of the structure of correct reasoning. The rules of inference in a system of logic may derive some of their interest from their proximity to the principles of actual human reasoning, but their justification can lie only in the fact that they preserve validity; that is, that from true premises they allow the inference only of a true conclusion.

Formal systems are built in such a way as to make the recognition of a valid inference as easy as possible on the basis of the form of the premises and of the conclusion. We may regard a system of symbolic logic, with a specified vocabulary and precise rules for forming sentences and drawing inferences, as a language. One of the purposes of such artificial languages is to avoid the vagueness and ambiguity inherent in a natural language, such as English or French. One of their main purposes is to allow a logician to translate putative inferences from natural languages into a symbolic language and thereby discover the formal criteria of validity for inferences in natural language. As we saw in Chapter I, these criteria are often summed up in the *form* or *logical form* of the natural language sentences involved.

When a sentence is translated from English into symbolic notation, it often loses some of the nuances it had in English, but, in return for this loss, its logical form is made clear and precise if the translation is an adequate one. A logician, then, may be concerned with the criteria which can be cited to support the claim that one symbolization of a given English sentence is better than another. The relations between a formal and a natural language raise questions that concern the logician as well as the philosopher of language. For example, in a symbolization, just how much of the meaning of a sentence may be sacrificed in the interests of an easier recognition of validity? Sometimes such questions lead to a reformulation of the system of logic in an attempt to incorporate into it some of the important features of natural language formerly left out of account.

In general, the difficulty of translating from natural languages to a logical language is greater than might first appear. Closeness to natural language is not the only virtue or the main virtue a logical system can possess. The clarity in displaying valid forms of argument and the comprehensiveness of the supply of arguments that can be expressed in a symbolic language are among its more important aims.

For this reason, logicians are also concerned with the general properties which characterize the inferences allowed in a system of symbolic logic. Among the most important properties of this kind are the *completeness* and the *soundness* of a system. To say that such a system is complete is to say that *all* the arguments which are semantically valid (which are such that it must be that if premises are true, then the conclusion is true) can be shown to be syntactically valid (the conclusion can be derived from the premises within the rules of the system). To say the system is sound is to say that *only* semantically valid inferences are allowed by the rules.

Problems of completeness and soundness illustrate the extent to which logic, which was characterized above as a study of the forms of correct reasoning, depends on the study of semantic or model theoretic questions; that is, questions concerning the relationships of a language to what it represents or can represent. For the validity of an inference means preservation of truth, and truth is a matter of certain relations of sentences to what they refer to or stand for.

For further insight into the study of logic, the reader should refer to Chapters I and II and should also see section 6 (below) on philosophy of mathematics.

6. *Philosophy of Mathematics*

Like philosophers of science and of history, philosophers of mathematics have been concerned with both the methods and the subject matter of the discipline that they study. Most people achieve some proficiency in elementary mathematics without ever questioning the nature of numbers themselves. The philosopher of mathematics considers such questions, asking whether numbers are objects, concepts, properties of sets of objects, or perhaps sets. Further, the philosopher asks what sort of evidence, if any, is relevant to mathematical assertions. A child may become acquainted with numbers by first being shown one orange, then two, then three. But this does not show that arithmetical truths are empirical. Rather, one can argue that mathematical propositions are analytic, since it seems that they can be proven by logical and set-theoretical considerations alone. But if we argue that mathematical propositions are analytic and hence have no extralogical content, we are then faced with the problem of accounting for the apparent relevance of mathematics to the empirical world.

On the other hand, if we hold that mathematical truths are synthetic, we must account for their apparent necessity —for the apparent incoherence inherent in the denial of a truth of mathematics.

Philosophers of mathematics have inquired into the notion of a set, investigating the consistency of intuitive set theory and seeking to determine whether set theory can be reduced to logic. The relation between numbers and sets is also a matter for investigation. Is it possible, for example, to define numbers in terms of sets? If so, what is to be gained by so doing?

Some of these questions lead us to ask just what would constitute good reasons for believing that mathematical propositions are in fact either analytic or synthetic. Such a question has to do with what constitutes a proof *about* mathematics. But we can also ask what constitutes a proof *within* mathematics. And the question of what constitutes such a proof is as much a question of logic as of philosophy of mathematics. Thus, for this among other reasons, the philosophy of mathematics is inseparable from the study of formal logic.

7. Philosophy of Science

There are many notions used in science that the scientist, in the capacity of a scientist, does not usually analyze. There are presuppositions that he or she cannot be expected either to make explicit or to justify. Nor does the scientist typically investigate the nature of scientific method, of scientific theory, or of scientific knowledge and the propositions of science. The philosopher of science, however, may be expected to undertake just such tasks as these.

It is obvious that a great deal of material is common to epistemology and the philosophy of science. Among the scientist's presuppositions must surely be some belief in the possibility of empirical knowledge. And any discussion of the nature of a scientific theory will include the question of confirmation and the notions of induction and probability.

Currently, much discussion in the philosophy of science centers around the problems of explanation and prediction. In order for one to be able to explain a particular phenomenon, must a statement of its occurrence be capable of being deduced from causal laws and from some statements about causal conditions? Is an explanation of this deductive form typical of scientific explanations? Is there only one logical form for an acceptable explanation? What lies behind our conviction that it is a better explanation of a baby's having blue eyes that his parents have blue eyes than that his mother ate blueberries during her pregnancy? Or, in general, why is science preferable to augury? Similar questions may be asked about predictions. What must be the logical form of a prediction if it is to be justified? And what is the relation between the form of an explanation and that of a prediction?

Questions about explanation and prediction are among the many that give rise to questions about causality. What does it mean when a doctor says that an antibiotic injection can have many different effects? An introduction to the kind of interest a philosopher may have in this question is presented in Chapter VII. Philosophers have been interested in what it means to say that a particular event A caused another event B. Does such an assertion imply that there is a general law about events like A causing events like B? Questions like this present a natural introduction to an inquiry into the nature of scientific laws. One may ask why some general statements are laws—for example, Mendel's law of genetics—while other true general statements are not—for example, 'All children's shoes purchased in California in 1962 cost more than 5 cents per pair when new.'

What is the justification for theories that bear no obvious relation to everyday experience and for the introduction of such terms as 'atom', 'proton', 'neutron', and 'electron'? What is the relation between theories involving concepts such as these and the experimental results that these theories purport to explain? And what, if any, are the implications of such theories for philosophical inquiry generally? For example, philosophers have often discussed the concept of time and have used and discussed the notion of simultaneity. What relevance has Einstein's theory of time to such a discussion? Or again, Heisenberg's uncertainty principle entails that in some respects the future cannot be predicted even on the basis of the best possible information about the past and present. Is this principle relevant to the philosopher's discussion of determinism and free will? In general we may say that it has been a philosophical question whether science and philosophy constitute different methods of studying the same subject matter or whether the subject matters of the two fields are quite independent of each other.

It has been suggested that the decision of a scientist in preferring one theory or hypothesis to others can be studied in the same way as other human decisions are studied. One prominent approach to decisions in general is to view them as attempts to maximize certain 'goods', usually called 'utilities'. To what extent does this model apply to a scientist's decisions? If it does apply, what are the scientist's utilities? It has been suggested that a scientist, when acting as a scientist, has only one utility: information. If so, what is this information? How is the expected information promised by a hypothesis related to the probability (degree of confirmation) of this hypothesis? One prominent philosopher of science has claimed that the two are inversely related; is he right? Is there only one kind of information relevant to a scientist's decisions, or are there several different sorts of information? To what extent are a scientist's decisions guided by values ('utilities') other than merely information?

This last question can be generalized beyond the decision theoretic framework. It has often been assumed that factual claims are more easily verified than value claims, that only factual claims have a place in science, and that the factual results of an experiment are brought into question if they depend on value judgments. Philosophers of science have questioned these assumptions; they have asked whether a scientist, in the role of scientist, makes value judgments, and, if so, what effects these judgments have on the status of the experimental results.

A group of questions, all of which have recently attracted intensive attention among philosophers of science, concerns transitions from one theory to another. When the theory in question is a large-scale one, such as Newtonian physics replacing Aristotelian physics, one can speak of scientific revolutions. Can they be characterized in cognitive terms, or do they involve value judgments? Is the work which leads to a scientific revolution structurally different from normal science? More generally, what is the typical structure of a scientific theory, and how does it change when a science progresses? Are changes in theory typically brought about by new evidence or by new problems? In discussing such questions, philosophers of science have often found themselves calling on material from the history of science to support their claims. It is a philosophical question, however, whether such historical evidence is ultimately relevant to purely philosophical theses, and if so, how.

8. *Philosophy of Language*

We use language to communicate with one another; our being able to do so seems to presuppose that at least some of the words in our language have meanings we understand and that our understanding is quite similar. But just what is the meaning of a word? And how does a word come to have the meaning it has? These are two general questions with which the philosophy of language is concerned.

In discussing ethics, we noted that it was not concerned with evaluating particular acts and, similarly, that epistemology was not concerned with compiling evidence for particular claims. An analogous disclaimer is in order for philosophy of language: In general, it is not the task of a philosopher investigating language to discover the meanings of particular words but rather to inquire into the relations among a word, its sense, its reference, the language in which it is a word, the users of that language, and the actions they can perform using language. In the course of this inquiry, philosophers may well attempt to analyze some terms that are essential in the philosophical study of language, among them, 'meaning', 'truth', and 'synonymy'.

One of the basic facts about language is that it is possible to understand a sentence we have never seen before if we understand the words used to make up the sentence. So philosophers of language have been concerned to investigate the way in which the meaning of words contributes to the meaning of those sentences in which the words are used.

The topics discussed in Chapter IV are illustrative of problems in philosophy of language. To what extent can the workings of a language be understood in terms of the extensions of its expressions? Can the intensions of words and phrases be identified with their meanings? What kinds of entities are meanings, anyway? Are possible worlds semanticists right in identifying meanings or intensions with functions from possible worlds to extensions? If not, why does this theory fail? And what is the true relation of extensions to intensions? These questions are so central to any comprehensive theory of language that it is not surprising to find that one version of possible worlds semantics has attracted considerable attention among theoretical linguists.

A major endeavor in the philosophy of language has been the search for a formal definition of truth, which neither leads to contradictions nor conflicts with our strong intuition that any sentence Φ is true if and only if the state of affairs described by Φ is the case. Some philosophers of language go so far as to claim that the best we can do in a theory of meaning is to study the truth conditions of the different kinds of sentences in our language. A satisfactory theory of truth might thus yield also a theory of meaning. Since we saw in Chapter IV that the concept of truth is closely related to the extensions of the different expressions of our language, a theory of meaning which focuses on truth conditions may thus be expected to make heavy use of the extensions of the different kinds of linguistic expressions.

An important role has been played in the philosophy of language and in the methodology of linguistics by the three-way division of the field of language theory into syntax, semantics, and pragmatics. As was indicated at the start of Chapter III, in *syntax* one is studying only the interrelations of various linguistic expressions. In *semantics*, one studies their representative relations to the part or aspect of reality these expressions can be used to describe. In *pragmatics*, one studies the way in which the sentences and other expressions are used, not just in speaking or writing but in one's dealings with one's environment.

Some linguists have emphasized the independence of these three types of studies, especially the autonomy of syntax. It is nevertheless clear that the three are related. Language users must garner the meanings of their sentences from syntactical clues. Semantical relations are not natural relations that could, for example, be directly perceived. They are established and maintained through certain rule-governed human activities, which belong to the province of pragmatics. Semantic relations, we may thus suggest, are based on pragmatic ones.

An extreme form of this dependence of semantics on pragmatics is Wittgenstein's theory of what he calls *language games* as the basis of linguistic meaning. Language games are for Wittgenstein rule-governed activities involving language. Other philosophers of language have restricted the term 'pragmatics' to the study of the contributions made by the nonlinguistic context of the utterance of a sentence to its meaning. The relevant features of this context may include the time of the utterance, the speaker, and the person to whom the utterance is addressed. So conceived, pragmatics is little more than the semantics of context dependence.

The emphasis in recent years on logic and the analytic method of philosophy has no doubt stimulated interest in the problems of philosophy of language. Further, recent work in empirical linguistics, including the theory of transformational grammars, has increased philosophical inquiry directed at criticizing and describing the basic assumptions and methods of linguistic science and at applying the insights of linguists, where possible, to traditional philosophical problems. But like questions in other areas of philosophy, many of those in philosophy of language—such as "What is the meaning of 'truth'?"—have been discussed since the time of Plato and Aristotle.

9. Philosophy of Mind

Philosophy of mind, as a separate area of philosophical inquiry, has not played as prominent a role in the history of philosophy as ethics or epistemology. But this is not to say that the problems in this area have only recently come to be discussed. Inquiry into the nature of intentional action, desire, and motivation is present throughout the history of philosophy.

In discussing ethics, we noted that some philosophers have attempted to define the rightness of an action in terms of the motives from which the agent acted. To talk about a person's motives, intentions, desires, or beliefs is to talk about something mental or psychological. In order to gain some insight into the nature of these mental phenomena, philosophers have investigated the logical structure of the sentences used to describe motives, beliefs, and the like. Typically, such sentences are intensional (see Chapter V). Some philosophers of mind feel that intensionality is the most distinctive feature of discourse about psychological phenomena, and they have devoted their energies to a detailed study of the logical properties of intensional sentences.

The analysis of the concept of belief is another important problem in this area. Is the expression of beliefs to be taken as conclusive evidence of what one believes? The familiar saying that actions speak louder than words finds an analogue in the philosophical argument that what someone does must be taken as final evidence of what she or he believes. Others have argued that it is not enough to say that a person's actions are *evidence* of his or her beliefs (or desires or intentions); rather that these mental notions have no meaning except that which can be defined in terms of a person's behavior or physical responses to stimuli. Such problems of the relation of mind to body, of the mental to the physical, have played an important role in philosophy, particularly since Descartes.

Closely related to the concepts we have been discussing (such as motive and desire) is the concept of intentional action. So much philosophical inquiry has been focused on this concept in recent years that it would not be amiss to treat "philosophy of action" as a separate field. But to do so would be to de-emphasize the close connection between the problems involved in the analysis of action and other problems in the philosophy of mind.

What is the nature of action? How, for example, can the things a person does be distinguished from the things that happen to one? What is the relation between an action's being intentional and its being voluntary? And further, what is the distinction between someone's *deciding* to do something and *predicting* that he or she will do it? All these are questions arising from the attempt to analyze the concept of action.

In addition, philosophers of mind have attempted to clarify the distinction between a person's *reasons* for acting as he or she does and the *causes* of the action. Are a person's beliefs, desires, and motives reasons for that person's actions, or causes of them, or both?

It may seem difficult to distinguish the philosopher's task from the psychologist's. But the philosopher is not an empirical scientist. The relations the philosopher seeks among the concepts we have referred to are not connections one could discover in a laboratory. The philosopher seeks to make an analysis of such concepts as believing, desiring, and intending that will make clear the logical relations between them. For example, most philosophers hold that it is a logical presupposition of a person's intending to do something that the person believes it is possible to do it. The philosopher's evidence is not that people usually, or even always, believe they can do what they intend to do. Rather, the evidence comes from an analysis of the concepts, and the claim is that part of what it *means* to intend to do something is that one believes one can do it.

10. Philosophy of History

The philosopher of history studies history in much the same way as the philosopher of science studies science. One may ask just what history is; for example, whether it is essential to history that historians interpret past events or attempt to discover patterns in history. Historians typically attempt to *explain* events and people's actions, and historical explanations have received as much attention from philosophers as have scientific explanations. Are historical explanations *causal* explanations? Are the requirements for an acceptable explanation in history different from those in science? The objects of historical study are primarily human actions and events as they influence and affect people; does this fact influence the kind of explanation that is appropriate? Does an explanation that gives the reasons for a person's action also give the causes? Is it a sufficient explanation for an action to give a person's reasons? What role does the notion of "law" play in history? Are there historical laws at all? Do the criteria for a law in history differ from those in science; could it be a historical law that a hungry people is a people bent on revolution?

A philosopher may also investigate the role that historical evidence plays in predictions. Does the logical form of the prediction of an event in the history of man parallel the logical form of a scientific prediction? There seem to be many ways in which the method of historians differs from that of scientists. To ask what history is is to ask in part whether history is a science. Do the differences between history and science cast doubt on the validity of history as a source of knowledge, or are the differences simply a product of different subject matter?

The question of evidence or good reasons recurs throughout philosophy, and philosophy of history is no exception. Historians often offer theories of history to account for the past, theories that may, for example, purport to show a pattern in past events. If two such theories conflict, what would constitute evidence in favor of either? Does the past itself provide evidence? Events in the past are in principle unobservable; they have already occurred. The philosopher of history shares with the epistemologist an interest in how or whether it is possible to have knowledge of the past. Does memory provide us with evidence about the past, or does the fact that one can believe he or she remembers something that did not actually occur invalidate evidence from memory?

11. Philosophy of Religion

Philosophy of religion is not theology, nor is it a body of religious beliefs. Rather, it is a critical investigation of the meaning and justification of religious statements. Just as the philosopher may ask what constitutes scientific evidence, it may also be asked what constitutes evidence for religious belief. While it is generally agreed, however, that scientific knowledge must be justified by appeal to evidence, it has been asked not only whether there *can* be evidence for religious propositions but also whether such propositions stand in need of supporting evidence.

Philosophers have inquired into just what kind of propositions the propositions of religion are. If they purport to give information about the world, they are not analytic. But if they are synthetic, on what grounds is one to confirm or deny them? Can revelation be a source of evidence? A distinction has often been made between revealed theology, by which this question is answered affirmatively, and rational or natural theology. Natural theology begins with evidence from the world or nature as we find it; it is said to be rational because its method is that of argument from purported facts about the world to claims about the existence and the nature of a divine being. If this distinction is correctly drawn, is there any reason to hold that one of these kinds of belief is better justified than the other?

Since the Middle Ages, when many philosophers were theologians as well, part of the philosophy of religion has been concerned with purported proofs for the existence of God. Are any proofs possible? The so-called ontological argument purports to deduce that God exists, not from empirical facts, but merely from an analysis of the concept of God. Many other arguments for the existence of God may be offered as well: An argument from design may be based on the claim that God must exist in order to account for the order in the universe. In giving a causal argument, one may hold that since everything that exists must have a cause, and the universe exists, then something must be the cause of the universe; and only God could be the cause of the universe. Finally, one may offer a moral argument to show that only in terms of God's existence can we explain moral values. But each of these arguments is open to serious objections of various sorts. Thus the philosopher of religion may ask whether these arguments can be defended against the objections, modified so as to avoid them, or supplanted by new arguments that are not open to objection.

The question of whether God exists or not is closely related to the question of the nature or attributes of God. If we merely assert that God exists but refuse to attempt to describe His nature, then the assertion of existence can be of no real interest. But if we attempt to describe His nature, then a host of new problems arises. If, for example, God is said to be omniscient, omnipotent, and benevolent, then the existence of evil poses a major difficulty. If God is omniscient, He knows about evil; if He is omnipotent, He can eliminate it; if He is benevolent, He opposes evil. Yet evil exists; must God therefore lack one of these three properties of omnipotence, omniscience, and benevolence? Such problems are typical of those in the philosophy of religion.

Not all philosophers, of course, have been concerned with statements about a god within the Judaeo-Christian tradition. Some have argued that while man can prove the existence of a god, it is one that differs significantly from the God of Western tradition. Others claim to be able to prove that no god exists; still others deny the meaningfulness of all claims about the existence of any being which cannot be verified empirically.

12. Political Philosophy

Political philosophy consists essentially of inquiry into the relationship between individuals in a governed society and the government of that society. Unlike much of political science, it is not especially concerned with the description and analysis of existing governments. Rather, it is mainly concerned with examining the reasons for having any government at all and considering, in the light of those reasons, the justifiability of various features that governments may have. Thus the political philosopher is likely to ask what general form the political organization of society should take. In seeking to answer this question, the philosopher will be faced with the task of considering the nature of human beings and the functions and purposes of social organization.

Thomas Hobbes, for example, begins his treatise on political philosophy, *Leviathan*, with a discussion of the nature of man, arguing that in the absence of political organizations life is "solitary, poor, nasty, brutish, and short" and that it is the function of political organization to provide men with a way of "getting themselves out from that miserable condition." He then goes on to consider, in the light of these views, what form the political organization of society should take.

Once a view of the nature of man and the function of political organization has been accepted, the question of the proper form of government involves many other philosophically interesting issues. What, for example, is the proper relation between law and morality? Some have argued that the body of laws in a society must reflect the moral attitudes that predominate in the society. Others hold that morality is essentially outside the law and that consequently it is inappropriate for legislation to be concerned with matters of morality at all. Rather, they argue, law results from an attempt by organized society to limit individual or group freedom, only insofar as its unrestricted exercise would injure individuals or groups within the society.

A related question, which is equally basic, concerns the procedure within the state for establishing and changing laws. When an individual is a member of a governed society, he is, it seems, committed to abide by its laws. What, then, are the rights and obligations of the citizen who considers a law to be unjustifiable? One can argue, for example, that it was wrong for citizens of Nazi Germany to obey Hitler's genocidal laws. But on what grounds was it wrong? Is it because obedience to those laws was a violation of some natural law? Such is the view that some philosophers have held. But then the question of the possibility of natural law must be considered, and new problems arise when we ask how natural laws, if there can be any, are discoverable.

Such questions about the nature and function of political organization are obviously inseparable from questions about the nature and function of laws. Hence there are strong interdependencies between political philosophy and philosophy of law. But there are differences nonetheless, and in recent years philosophy of law has come increasingly to be regarded as a separable field of study. (See section 14 of this chapter.)

13. *History of Philosophy*

The distinctions we have thus far suggested within the body of philosophy have been based on typical questions from each area. However, one may also regard philosophy through its chronological development, in the study of the history of philosophy. It is difficult to say exactly what constitutes a historical study of philosophy. For example, one who studies what philosophers during the seventeenth and eighteenth centuries wrote about epistemological questions soon becomes involved in criticism and evaluation—that is, in epistemological inquiry. Yet one is also engaged in a historical study. And any purported epistemological study that does not take cognizance of the writings of past philosophers is simply not a thorough study. The problems of philosophy have not changed as much as, for instance, those of science; therefore, attention to past writings is not peripheral to contemporary philosophy, as it often is to contemporary science. In this sense, there is always reason for attention to history in philosophy.

One approach to a historical study of philosophy is, as we have mentioned above, to study those writings from a particular period of time that are concerned with selected problems. But many other approaches are possible. One can also study the writings of some one philosopher about many problems. In so doing, one may be interested in the effect that the philosopher's metaphysical arguments have had on his epistemological or ethical position. Are the positions he takes on various questions consistent with one another? Do his metaphysical presuppositions conflict with his epistemological claims? In the course of such an inquiry it may be useful to classify a philosopher as, for example, a materialist or an idealist, a rationalist or an empiricist. Such classification is no end in itself, of course, but it may provide insight into the influence that previous philosophers have had on a writer and into his influence on subsequent writers. It must be kept in mind that when we say that two philosophers are, for example, empiricists, we are saying that in some respects their positions are alike. But it is just as important to recognize the respects in which their positions differ.

Philosophers have never lived in a vacuum; their writings have always been influenced by the writings of other philosophers, as well as by the society in which they live. It is often useful to study one philosopher in the light of some preceding philosophical writings of which he takes cognizance in his writings. In this way, one may come to have a clearer grasp of the problems to which the philosopher has addressed himself and may thus be better able to understand his writings. A historian of philosophy is often interested in the fact that problems of a particular kind predominate in the writings of a given period. For example, Greek philosophy before Socrates was primarily concerned to discover the fundamental stuff of which the universe was composed. But with the philosophy of Socrates came a notable change in focus from human environment to persons and their relations with others. To a philosopher, the questions that have been asked in philosophy are often as interesting as the answers that have been given.

14. New Directions

Some of the questions discussed by philosophers and some of the areas of study which are included within philosophy have been a part of philosophy throughout its recorded history. Others have been raised because philosophers have long attended to those questions concerning the human condition which are most pressing in their time. Just as Plato's concern with the nature of the ideal state reflected the strong interests of his time, so many philosophers of today turn their attention to questions that are brought to the fore by contemporary social developments as well as by changes in what we know and in what we have the capability to do.

In some cases, the results of this study are to be seen in shifting orientation in historically well-identified areas of philosophy. The capabilities that result from increased genetic research, for instance, raise significant ethical issues. And the data concerning genetic encoding of information provide a broadened context within which epistemologists and philosophers of science continue to study the long-discussed concept of information.

In other cases, the results of shifts in the direction of philosophers' attention are to be seen in the development of new areas of study within philosophy. These new areas may draw from previous work throughout philosophy, they may demark a set of questions which has been a part of an established area of study in philosophy as worthy of attention in its own right, and they may challenge the assumptions and the methodology which have characterized earlier work in philosophy. Of these newly identified areas of study in philosophy, we mention only three.

PHILOSOPHY OF MEDICINE

The philosophy of medicine is concerned with the philosophical aspects of the practices, policies, and institutions that are related in fundamental ways to health and medicine. These philosophical issues fall mainly into two categories: issues in medical ethics and issues of a conceptual or methodological sort. Questions of medical ethics are those involving the moral dimensions of decision making in medical contexts and in contexts related to the biological sciences—including the full spectrum of activities pertaining to the provision of health care. These range from specific clinical interactions between care provider and patient, on the one hand, to social policy decisions about medical research, public health programs, and the structuring and financing of health care delivery systems on the other hand. Typical of such concerns are the familiar questions pertaining to abortion, euthanasia, and rights regarding reproduction. But these specifically medical questions are addressed within the philosophy of medicine in terms of the underlying philosophical concepts, such as personal autonomy, personhood, freedom of action, and personal dignity. Ethical questions also arise in regard to the methods and objectives of research involving human beings as subjects or threatening the welfare of human beings because of characteristics of the product or the process of the research.

Those questions in the philosophy of medicine which lie outside the range of medical ethics include epistemological issues, such as questions of evidence and predictability in clinical contexts, and also questions of methodology which fall within the domain of the philosophy of science. What, for example, counts as adequate evidence that a treatment is effective? What justifies the claim—indeed, what does the claim mean—that a treatment is safe? How much can we learn about humans by conducting research with nonhuman animals, and what distinguishes valid interspecies extrapolation from invalid extrapolation?

Some questions seem to be a blend of both conceptual and ethical concerns. What, for instance, is health? Is the concept value-free, or must we incorporate ethical judgments in deciding what counts as healthy? Conversely, what is disease? Are the concepts of health and disease primarily biological, or psychological? And how are these concepts related to that of the normal state of an organism?

PHILOSOPHY OF LAW

The law surrounds us; at once, it enriches and constrains us all. Philosophy of law is the attempt to understand the law from the philosophical point of view—to gain insight into its objectives and justifications, its processes, its variants both actual and ideal, and its relationships to other social institutions.

Perhaps the most familiar questions in the philosophy of law are those that concern the relationship between law and morality. Is there a moral obligation to obey the law? Is civil disobedience justifiable? What relationships exist between legal rights and moral obligation, or between legality and justice? Should all immoral action be made illegal? But these questions cannot be properly considered except in the context of an understanding of what law is. Hence they lead us to consider more fundamental questions.

What is a legal system? Must a system contain certain goals or principles, or satisfy certain moral criteria, in order to be a legal system at all, or to be a legitimate legal system? What are its objectives in fact, and what might they be? What relationship does a legal system bear to government and to social institutions such as those of private property, the contract, or basic rights and freedoms? By what criteria should such legal systems be evaluated, and how, in particular, do contemporary legal systems—such as the adversary system most familiar to us—fare as judged by such criteria?

Philosophers of law explore such questions in order to gain a deeper understanding of legal systems in general and of our legal system in particular. They examine basic concepts that play an important role in legal argumentation—such as the concepts of precedent, reasonable doubt, and due process, and they also examine the use within the law of concepts of broader application—such as the concepts of causation, responsibility, and mental competence. Further, they examine, describe, and evaluate the standards and processes according to which arguments are accepted or rejected within the legal system.

Not all philosophers of law agree about what law is—about what makes a given rule or principle a part of a legal system, or about what relationships exist among the various agencies that are involved in the establishment and operation of a legal system—the legislature, the judiciary, the executive and enforcement agencies, and the legal profession. Competing theories of what a legal system is, and of how it works, are thus a part of the subject matter of philosophy of law.

Recently, there has also been increased interest in exploring the relationships between the legal system on the one hand and economic and social forces on the other; the philosophy of law thus incorporates considerations of issues in economics, political theory, and the history of social change.

Finally, some consideration of problems of ethics and professional responsibility in the practice of law may be included within the philosophy of law. These problems include such issues as the origin and limits of the lawyer's obligation to serve the interests of the client, and the extent of the responsibilities that derive from the lawyer's various roles as officer of the court, advocate of the client, member of the professional guild, and citizen.

In any event, study of the philosophy of law is not training in the law. It is philosophy, focusing on the law, and reflecting on it in the larger context of social, political, and ethical considerations.

PHILOSOPHY OF FEMINISM

The movement for women's liberation—in all its diversity—is one among many recent sources of social challenge and social change, and this movement raises many issues which are of philosophical interest. In some cases, the questions raised have long been discussed within philosophy. For instance, the role of maternal, paternal, and fetal rights in abortion is not a new subject of philosophical attention. Nor is inquiry into the concept of equality. However, attention to such questions and interest in them have surely been sparked by social pressures from the feminist movement.

Some questions which one might consider in a course in philosophical issues in feminism could have been asked independently of recent social developments, but they had not been. For instance, does the concept of a minority apply to women in twentieth century America? Women are a numerical majority of the population, and women are not socialized exclusively or even primarily by women. How are these facts to be taken into account in understanding the status of women as a minority group?

Philosophers have long directed their attention to the question of the best use of data from empirical research. But in particular it has been in the philosophical study of feminist issues that questions have been raised concerning the consequences for social policy, if any, of data concerning sex-linked endocrinological differences and of data concerning developmental differences between females and males. The question of what would count as evidence that such differences are biological in their origin or that they result primarily from sociological conditions is also a subject of interest.

There is no question that within the history of philosophy, most philosophers have been men. There is a significant question as to how that fact has been reflected in the arguments, evidence, conclusions, and even questions studied. Just as some historians claim that generalizations about the

American character depend on considering only adult male Americans, some philosophers argue that discussions of humans and the human condition have been biased by the fact that the discussants were men taking men to be paradigms of humans.

Feminist philosophy and the philosophy of feminism converge on many points, but there are differences as well. The former refers to philosophical positions on the basis of which many people—male and female alike—regard themselves as feminists. Just as, for example, Marxists—despite differences among them—can be expected to advocate some philosophical positions in common, so also feminist philosophers can be expected to advocate certain conclusions and address their attention to certain arguments. The philosophy of feminism— that is, the philosophical study of issues related to feminism— need not support or attack feminism, any more than the philosophy of science need support or attack the substantive positions and research priorities of scientists. Some feminists support, for example, reverse discrimination; it is incumbent on them to provide the strongest arguments possible in its defense. Reverse discrimination and special opportunities for members of groups which have received discriminatory treatment, and the arguments which can be offered pro and con, are all topics for analysis and evaluations in the philosophy of feminism.

15. Conclusion

Three points about the divisions within the body of philosophy must be emphasized. First, the areas are not independent of one another; rarely is any study in philosophy irrelevant to any other study in philosophy. Arguments in one area may be presupposed by the discussion of a problem, or even its formulation, in another. If, for example, in the philosophy of science, one is investigating different methods for the confirmation of theories, he or she must have in mind some criterion for the adequacy of evidence. One may even attack the problem by first attempting to discover the epistemological assumptions of various methods of confirmation.

Second, it must not be assumed that the areas of inquiry discussed in this chapter are the sole province of the professional philosopher. Practicing scientists, for example, often seek to formulate and answer some of the questions here identified as philosophical, and some of the most creative work in logic has been done by mathematicians. It is a common mistake, fostered in part by the division of research areas in the modern university, to suppose that philosophic concerns and problems are completely separate from the concerns of scientists, lawyers, artists, physicians, and so on.

Third, the demarcation of areas in philosophy is neither an exhaustive nor an unchanging classification. It is often neither possible nor important to decide to what area of inquiry a particular question belongs. Is the question of the tenability of the analytic–synthetic distinction an epistemological question or one for the philosophy of language? This question is moot, but inquiry into the analytic–synthetic distinction in no way presupposes any answer to this question. Some questions in philosophy underlie several specific studies: The question of the logical structure of explanations is as relevant to the philosophy of science as it is to the philosophy of history. And specific studies of historical and scientific explanations in turn shed light on the more general question of the nature of explanation.

This chapter will have served the purpose for which it was intended if the reader has gained from it some insight into the general problems to which philosophers have addressed themselves and is thereby better able to understand his or her readings in philosophy as well as to plan for further study and work in philosophy.

Solutions to Selected Exercises

Solutions to Selected Exercises

Following are solutions, or in some cases partial solutions, to selected exercises. The exercises for which solutions are provided here are marked at the end of each chapter with an asterisk (*). Some of the solutions below are accompanied by explanatory remarks. It is of course not expected that students will explain their answers as we have sometimes done below. But these comments may provide helpful ways in which to think about some of the exercises.

Chapter I. Elementary Logic

Exercise 3 (partial solution)

Note: There are 32 such profiles. Arguments can be found to correspond to 15 of these. Below are two profiles, an argument corresponding to the first, and an explanation of why there can be no argument corresponding to the second.

F	Carter is President and Nixon is a Senator (premise 1)
T	Carter is President (premise 2)
T	Nixon is not a Senator (conclusion)
I	
U	

F	For either of two reasons, no argument can correspond
T	to this profile: No invalid (I) argument is sound (S), and
T	no argument with a false premise (F) is sound (S).
I	
S	

Exercise 5

P	Q	~Q	(P & ~Q)	(P → Q)	~(P & ~Q)	[~(P & ~Q)↔(P → Q)] is a tautology
T	T	F	F	T	T	T
T	F	T	T	F	F	T
F	T	F	F	T	T	T
F	F	T	F	T	T	T

Exercise 9 (*partial solution*)

     9a.   (P → Q)
     9d.   ~(P & ~Q)

Exercise 10 (*partial solution*)

      10c.   P: Helen will camp.
           Q: The moon is full.

$$(Q \to P) \,\&\, (\sim Q \to \,\sim P)$$

To arrive at a symbolization for 10c, we must spell out the elliptical "otherwise not." Otherwise than what, not what? If it is otherwise than that *the moon is full*, then it is not that *Helen will camp*. While this intermediate step is not idiomatic English, such sentences may help us arrive at a symbolic sentence which has the same truth conditions. Our symbolic sentence is logically equivalent to $(Q \leftrightarrow P)$, but the English sentence we are symbolizing contains "but" as well as obvious phrases of negation. Had we symbolized the English sentence as a biconditional, these English structural parts would not have been represented in the symbolic sentence. In general the first requirement of an adequate symbolization is that it have the same truth conditions, to the extent that we can reflect them in the symbolism, as the sentence we are symbolizing. But since logically equivalent sentences have the same truth conditions, this first requirement provides no basis for selecting one among several logically equivalent sentences as a better symbolization than the others. So in choosing among logically equivalent symbolic sentences, it is usually best to prefer sentences that reflect as much of the formal structure of the English sentence as is possible within the symbolic language at one's disposal.

    10d.   P: All scholars ruminate.
           On the basis of this scheme of abbreviation, the symbolization of 10d is simply

       P

After the discussion of this chapter, it is apparent that there is important structure in 10d which is not captured by this symbolization. However, the symbolic language available to us at this stage is inadequate to reveal that structure. Consider this sentence again after you have studied Chapter II.

Chapter II. Predicate Calculus and Sets

Exercise 2 (partial solution)

    2a.   Scheme of abbreviation:

$$G(_1): (_1) \text{ is a tall guard}$$
$$M(_1): (_1) \text{ is mistaken}$$
$$S(_1)(_2): (_1) \text{ is shorter than } (_2)$$
$$j: \text{John}$$
$$h: \text{Smith}$$
$$d: \text{Dokes}$$
$$c: \text{the coach}$$

On the basis of this scheme of abbreviation, 2a may be symbolized:

$$Gj \rightarrow (Shd \lor Mc)$$

An alternate scheme of abbreviation which replaces '$G(_1)$' with

$$T(_1): (_1) \text{ is tall}$$
$$R(_1): (_1) \text{ is a guard}$$

leads to a symbolization which is liable to difficulties. See exercise 3 of this chapter.

2d. On the basis of the scheme of abbreviation

$$L(_1): (_1) \text{ is a philosopher}$$
$$P(_1): (_1) \text{ is a problem}$$
$$T(_1)(_2): (_1) \text{ thinks about } (_2)$$

2d may be symbolized as:

$$(x)(Lx \rightarrow (\exists y)(Py \ \& \ Txy))$$

2e. On the basis of the scheme of abbreviation

$$P(_1): (_1) \text{ is a person}$$
$$H(_1): (_1) \text{ is at home}$$

either of the following sentences is an acceptable symbolization of 2e:

$$(x) \ (Px \rightarrow \ \sim Hx)$$
$$\sim (\exists x) \ (Px \ \& \ Hx)$$

This scheme of abbreviation takes into account the fact, sometimes ignored by logicians, that "no one", "someone", and the like are *personal* pronouns by including a predicate 'is a person.' However, this scheme of abbreviation would not allow one to reveal any structural relation between being at home and being at someone's home. An alternate scheme of abbreviation might be:

$$P(_1): (_1) \text{ is a person}$$
$$H(_1)(_2): (_1) \text{ is at } (_2)\text{'s home.}$$

On the basis of this scheme of abbreviation, either of the following sentences is an acceptable symbolization of 2e:

$$(x) (Px \rightarrow {\sim} Hxx)$$
$${\sim} (\exists x) (Px \ \& \ Hxx)$$

Exercise 3

Since the proposed symbolization is a conjunction, it is true just in case each of its conjuncts is true. Suppose that the English sentence is true. If the proposed symbolization meets the minimal criterion of acceptability, it too is true on this supposition. So each of its conjuncts is true. In particular 'Cg' is true and 'Sg' is true. Since each of these sentences is true on our supposition, so also their conjunction '(Cg & Sg)' is true. Since this conjunction is true whenever the proposed symbolization is true, the proposed symbolization logically implies '(Cg & Sg)'. Using the same scheme of abbreviation, this conjunction would be a symbolization of the English sentence 'Gerry is a clumsy surgeon', and the original English sentence surely does not imply this sentence! The symbolic sentence proposed as a symbolization is true only when '(Cg & Sg)' is true, and so the proposed symbolization has significantly different truth conditions than the English sentence.

Exercise 5 (partial solution)

5a: Everything is larger than something.
5b: Everything is such that something is larger than it.
5e: Something is larger than something.
5f: Something is such that something is larger than it.

Exercise 7

$\Lambda, \{1\}, \{2\}, \{3\}, \{1, 2\}, \{1, 3\}, \{2, 3\}, \{1, 2, 3\}$

Chapter III. Further Logical Notions

Exercise 3

Sentences (b), (c), (d), and (e) are true. The truth of (e) is less directly obvious than that of the others; its being true that R is a sufficient condition for its being true that P, and its being true that P is a sufficient condition for its being true that Q, and so (e) is true.

Exercise 6

A and B are mutually exclusive.
The following groups are jointly exhaustive:

A and B; A and C; A, B, and C.

Exercise 8, Part A

(a) line 2
(b) line 1
(c) line 3
(d) line 2
(e) line 2
(f) line 3
(g) line 4
(h) line 4
(i) line 1

Chapter IV. Truth and the Vehicles of Truth

Exercise 4

Both (a) and (b) are illustrations of two tokens of different types that express the same proposition:

(a) Paper is flammable.
     Paper is flammable and paper is flammable.

(b) A book is expensive, unless it is a paperback.
     Unless a book is a paperback, it is expensive.

Chapter V. Extensions Versus Intensions

Exercise 2

(a) Jimmy Carter, Amy Carter's father, the President of the United States in 1978. The extension of the expression is the man, no matter how he is specified.

(b) Same answer as (a).

(c) The expression has no extension. No one was the King of France in 1978, and so there is no person or thing that is the extension of the expression.

Exercise 5

The following sentence paraphrases the *de dicto* reading of 5:

Mark believes the following: that the number of member nations in the United Nations is smaller than the number of member nations in the United Nations.

Each of the following sentences paraphrases a possible *de re* reading of 5:

(a) There is a number, n, which is the actual number of member nations in the United Nations, and Mark believes that the number of member nations in the United Nations is smaller than n.

(b) There is a number, n, and there is a number, m, such that n is the number of member nations in the United Nations, m is smaller than n, and Mark believes that the number of member nations in the United Nations is m.

Chapter VI. The Analytic–Synthetic and *A Priori–A Posteriori* Distinctions

Exercise 1 (*partial solution*)

Examples of an analytic sentence:
(a) Every professional woman is a woman.
(b) Siblings have the same parents.

Examples of an *a priori* false sentence:
(a) Some human is not a human.
(b) There is a barber who shaves all and only those barbers who do not shave themselves.

Exercise 5

(a) The claim is synthetic *a posteriori*. (But see the discussion of definition in Chapter VIII, section 1; there is much to be said in favor of rejecting the supposition on which 5(a) rests.)

(b) The original statement is synthetic *a posteriori*, given the redefinition. (But again it may be instructive to consider the discussion in Chapter VIII, section 1.)

Chapter VII.   Definition and Philosophical Analysis

Exercise 3

Consider the claim that there are no sea-animals that are mammals. The fact that there are whales is a counterexample to this claim and shows it to be false. We might also say that the fact that whales are mammals, in conjunction with the fact that whales are sea-animals, provides a counterexample; to speak in this way is to cite a counterexample and to offer some explanation of why it is a counterexample. And we might say simply that whales are counterexamples. The reader may refer also to Chapter I, section 2, where an invalid argument is offered as a counterexample to the claim that another argument with the same logical form is a valid argument.

Chapter VIII.   Reading and Writing Philosophy

Exercise 2

(a)   is false.
(b)   is false.
(c)   is false.
(d)   is false.
(e)   is true.

Exercise 5

No suggestion is made about the respects in which men and apes are alike, and porpoises are unlike both. Of course there are such respects—for instance, in being land animals. But only some likenesses would lend greater probability to the likeness of men and apes in regard to problem-solving abilities, or the absence of that likeness between man and porpoises. This is an argument by analogy, and as such it is suspicious because the analogies which do hold between apes and men, but not with porpoises, do not support the likeness or similarity alleged.

Bibliography

The following is a list of books and series that are of major importance in the development of analytic philosophy or are particularly helpful to the introductory student. Most are by contemporary British and American authors. No attempt has been made to provide an exhaustive bibliography of contemporary analytic philosophy, nor are many books included that were written prior to the twentieth century or outside the current Anglo-American philosophical tradition.

The branches of philosophy to which each work listed is primarily relevant are indicated by capital letters following each entry according to the following code: A—anthology; B—series; C—philosophy of language; D—metaphysics; E—epistemology; F—philosophy of science; G—ethics and theory of value; H—aesthetics; I—philosophy of law; J—philosophy of religion; K—philosophy of history; L—logic and philosophy of logic; M—philosophy of mind; N—history of philosophy; O—political and social philosophy.

Ammerman, Robert R. (ed.). *Classics of Analytic Philosophy.* New York: McGraw-Hill, 1965. (A)

Anscombe, G. E. M. *Intention.* 2nd ed. Oxford: Basil Blackwell, 1963. (E, G, M)

————, and P. T. Geach. *Three Philosophers.* Oxford: Basil Blackwell, 1961. (D, L, N)

Armstrong, D. M. *Perception and the Physical World.* New York: Humanities Press, 1961. (E, M)

Austin, J. L. *How to Do Things with Words.* Cambridge, Mass.: Harvard University Press, 1962. (C, E)

————. *Philosophical Papers.* Oxford: Clarendon Press, 1961. (C, E)

————. *Sense and Sensibilia.* Oxford: Clarendon Press, 1962. (E)

Paperback: New York: Oxford University Press, 1964 (Galaxy Books).

Ayer, A. J. *Language, Truth and Logic.* 2nd ed. London: Gollancz, 1946. (C, D, E, G, L)

Paperback: New York: Dover, 1952.

————. *The Problem of Knowledge.* New York: St. Martin's Press, 1956. (E, M)

Paperback: Baltimore: Penguin Books, 1962.

Baker, Robert, and Frederick Elliston (eds.). *Philosophy and Sex.* Buffalo: Prometheus, 1976. (A, G, O)

Beardsley, Elizabeth, and Monroe Beardsley (eds.). THE PRENTICE-HALL FOUNDATIONS OF PHILOSOPHY SERIES. Englewood Cliffs, N.J.: Prentice-Hall.

    Aldrich, Virgil. *Philosophy of Art.*

    Alston, William. *Philosophy of Language.*

    Barker, Stephen. *Philosophy of Mathematics.*

    Chisholm, Roderick. *Theory of Knowledge.*

    Dray, William. *Philosophy of History.*

    Feinberg, Joel. *Political Philosophy.*

    Frankena, William. *Ethics.*

    Golding, Martin. *Philosophy of Law.*

    Hempel, Carl. *Philosophy of Natural Science.*

    Hick, John. *Philosophy of Religion.*

    Hull, David. *Philosophy of Biological Science.*

    McClellan, James. *Philosophy of Education.*

    Quine, Willard Van Orman. *Philosophy of Logic.*

    Rudner, Richard. *Philosophy of Social Science.*

    Salmon, Wesley. *Logic.*

    Shaffer, Jerome. *Philosophy of Mind.*

    Taylor, Richard. *Metaphysics.*

Berofsky, Bernard (ed.). *Free Will and Determinism.* New York: Harper & Row, 1966. (A, M, E)

Black, Max (ed.). CONTEMPORARY PHILOSOPHY. Ithaca, N.Y.: Cornell University Press. (B)

————, *Problems of Analysis.* Ithaca, N.Y.: Cornell University Press, 1954. (A)

Braybrooke, David (ed.). *Philosophical Problems of the Social Sciences.* London: Macmillan, 1965. (A, E, F)

Broad, C. D. *Five Types of Ethical Theory.* London: Routledge and Kegan Paul, 1930. (G, N)

Butler, R. J. (ed.). *Analytical Philosophy.* New York: Barnes & Noble, 1963. (A)

Carnap, Rudolf. *Logical Syntax of Language.* London: Routledge and Kegan Paul, 1937. (C, L)

————. *Meaning and Necessity*. Chicago: University of Chicago Press, 1942. (C, L)

————. *Philosophical Foundations of Physics*. Martin Gardner (ed.). New York: Basic Books, 1966. (E, F)

Castañeda, H.-N., and G. Nakhnikian (eds.). *Morality and the Language of Conduct*. Detroit: Wayne State University Press, 1963. (A, G)

Caton, Charles Edwin (ed.). *Philosophy and Ordinary Language*. Urbana: University of Illinois Press, 1963. (A, C)

Chappell, V. C. (ed.). *Ordinary Language*. Englewood Cliffs, N.J.: Prentice-Hall, 1964. (A, C)

————. *The Philosophy of Mind*. Englewood Cliffs, N.J.: Prentice-Hall, 1962 (paperback). (A, M)

Chisholm, Roderick M. *Perceiving*. Ithaca, N.Y.: Cornell University Press, 1957. (E, G)

Chomsky, Noam. *Language and Mind* (Enlarged edition). New York: Harcourt Brace Jovanovich, 1972. (C, M)

Danto, Arthur, and Sidney Morgenbesser (eds.). *Philosophy of Science*. New York: Meridian Books, 1960. (A, F)

Davidson, Donald, and Gilbert Harman (eds.). *The Logic of Grammar*. Encino, Calif.: Dickenson, 1975. (A, C, L)

Dray, William. *Laws and Explanation in History*. London: Oxford University Press, 1957. (F, K)

Elton, William (ed.). *Aesthetics and Language*. Oxford: Basil Blackwell, 1954. (A, H)

English, Jane (ed.). *Sex Equality*. Englewood Cliffs, N.J.: Prentice-Hall, 1977. (A, G, O)

Feigl, Herbert, *et al.* (eds.). MINNESOTA STUDIES IN THE PHILOSOPHY OF SCIENCE. Minneapolis: University of Minnesota Press. (A, B, F)

————, and Wilfrid Sellars (eds.). *Readings in Philosophical Analysis*. New York: Appleton-Century-Crofts, 1949. (A)

————, and May Brodbeck (eds.). *Readings in the Philosophy of Science*. New York: Appleton-Century-Crofts, 1953. (A, F)

————, Wilfrid Sellars, and Keith Lehrer. *New Readings in Philosophical Analysis*. New York: Appleton-Century-Crofts, 1972. (A)

Flew, Antony G. N. (ed.). *Essays in Conceptual Analysis*. London: Macmillan, 1956. (A, C, D, E, F, L)

———— (ed.). *Logic and Language* (First series). Oxford: Basil Blackwell, 1952. (A)

———— (ed.). *Logic and Language* (Second series). Oxford: Basil Blackwell, 1953. (A)

————, and Alasdair MacIntyre (eds.). *New Essays in Philosophical Theology*. London: SCM Press, 1955. (A, D, J)

————. *Thinking About Thinking*. Glasgow: William Collin, 1977. (C, E, L)

Fodor, Jerry, and Jerrold Katz (eds.). *The Structure of Language*. Englewood Cliffs, N.J.: Prentice-Hall, 1964. (A, C, L)

Gardiner, Patrick (ed.). *Theories of History*. Glencoe, Ill.: Free Press, 1959. (A, K)

Gombrich, E. H. *Art and Illusion*. New York: Bollingen Foundation, distributed by Pantheon Books, 1960. (H, E)

Goodman, Nelson. *Fact, Fiction and Forecast*. Cambridge, Mass.: Harvard University Press, 1955. (D, E, F)

Gould, Carol, and Marx Wartofsky (eds.). *Women and Philosophy*. New York: Putnam, 1976. (A, G, N, O)

Hacking, Ian. *Why Does Language Matter to Philosophy?* Cambridge: Cambridge University Press, 1975. (C, N)

Hampshire, Stuart. *Freedom and the Individual*. New York: Harper & Row, 1965. (D, E, G, M)

———. *Thought and Action*. London: Chatto & Windus, 1959. (D, E, M)

Hare, R. M. *Freedom and Reason*. Oxford: Clarendon Press, 1963. (G)

———. *The Language of Morals*. Oxford: Clarendon Press, 1952. (G) Paperback: New York: Oxford University Press, 1964 (Galaxy Books)

Harman, Gilbert. *Thought*. Princeton, N.J.: Princeton University Press, 1973. (C, E, M)

Hart, H. L. A. *The Concept of Law*. Oxford: Clarendon Press, 1961. (I)

———, and A. M. Honore. *Causation in the Law*. Oxford: Clarendon Press, 1959. (D, F, I)

Hempel, Carl G. *Fundamentals of Concept Formation in Empirical Science*. Chicago: University of Chicago Press, 1952. (F)

Hintikka, Jaakko. *Models for Modalities*. Dordrecht, Netherlands: Reidel, 1969. (C, D, E, L, M)

———. *The Intentions of Intentionality and Other New Models for Modalities*. Dordrecht, Netherlands: Reidel, 1975. (C, E, L, M)

Holland, R. F. (ed.). STUDIES IN PHILOSOPHICAL PSYCHOLOGY. London: Routledge and Kegan Paul; New York: Humanities Press. (B)

Honderich, Ted (ed.). INTERNATIONAL LIBRARY OF PHILOSOPHY AND SCIENTIFIC METHOD. London: Routledge and Kegan Paul; New York: Humanities Press. (B)

Hospers, John. *An Introduction to Philosophical Analysis*. Englewood Cliffs, N.J.: Prentice-Hall, 1963. (E, G)

Jeffrey, Richard C. *The Logic of Decision*. McGraw-Hill Series in Probability and Statistics. New York: McGraw-Hill, 1965. (E, F, G)

———. *Formal Logic: Its Scope and Its Limits*. New York: McGraw-Hill, 1967. (L)

Kalish, Donald, and Richard Montague. *Logic: Techniques of Formal Reasoning*. New York: Harcourt, Brace & World, 1964. (L)

Katz, Joseph, *et al.* (eds.). *Writers on Ethics*. Princeton, N.J.: Van Nostrand, 1962. (A, G)

Kaufmann, Walter Arnold. *Critique of Religion and Philosophy*. New York: Harper & Row, 1958. (G, J)

Kenny, Anthony. *Action, Emotion and Will*. London: Routledge and Kegan Paul, 1963. (E, G, M)

Kuhn, Thomas S. *The Structure of Scientific Revolutions*. Chicago: University of Chicago Press, 1962. (F)

Kyburg, Henry E., Jr., and Howard E. Smokler (eds.). *Studies in Subjective Probability*. New York: John Wiley, 1964. (A, F)

Lewis, C. I. *Mind and the World Order*. New York: Scribner, 1929. (D, E) Paperback: New York: Dover, 1956.

Lewis, David K. *Convention.* Cambridge, Mass.: Harvard University Press, 1969. (C)

Linsky, Leonard (ed.). *Semantics and the Philosophy of Language.* Urbana: University of Illinois Press, 1952. (A, C)

MacDonald, Margaret (ed.). *Philosophy and Analysis.* Oxford: Basil Blackwell, 1954. (A)

Margolis, Joseph (ed.). *Philosophy Looks at the Arts.* New York: Scribner, 1964. (A, H)

————. (ed.). *An Introduction to Philosophical Inquiry.* 2nd ed. New York: Knopf, 1978. (A)

Mates, Benson. *Elementary Logic.* New York: Oxford University Press, 1965. (L, C)

Melden, A. I. (ed.). *Essays in Moral Philosophy.* Seattle: University of Washington Press, 1958. (A, G)

———— (ed.). *Ethical Theories.* 2nd ed. Englewood Cliffs, N.J.: Prentice-Hall, 1961. (A, G)

Moore, G. E. *Principia Ethica.* Cambridge: Cambridge University Press, 1903. (G)

Paperback: Cambridge: Cambridge University Press, 1962.

Morgenbesser, Sidney, and James Walsh (eds.). *Free Will.* Englewood Cliffs, N.J.: Prentice-Hall, 1962. (A, G, M)

Morris, Herbert (ed.). *Freedom and Responsibility.* Stanford, Calif.: Stanford University Press, 1961. (A, G, I)

Mundle, C. W. K. *Perception: Facts and Theories.* London: Oxford University Press, 1971. (E)

Nagel, Ernest. *Principles of the Theory of Probability.* Chicago: University of Chicago Press, 1939. (F)

————. *The Structure of Science.* New York: Harcourt, Brace & World, 1961. (F)

————, and Richard B. Brandt (eds.). *Meaning and Knowledge.* New York: Harcourt, Brace & World, 1965. (A, E, C, D)

Nakhnikian, George. *An Introduction to Philosophy.* New York: Knopf, 1967. (C, E, F, G)

Neurath, Otto, Rudolf Carnap, and Charles Morris (eds.). INTERNATIONAL ENCYCLOPEDIA OF UNIFIED SCIENCE. Chicago: University of Chicago Press. (B)

Passmore, John A. *A Hundred Years of Philosophy.* 2nd ed. rev. London: Duckworth, 1966. (N)

Pears, David (ed.). *Freedom and the Will.* New York: St. Martin's Press, 1963. (A, D, G, I, M)

————. *Bertrand Russell and the British Tradition in Philosophy.* London: Fontana, 1967. (C, D, E, N)

Pitcher, George (ed.). *Truth.* Englewood Cliffs, N.J.: Prentice-Hall, 1964. (A, C, L)

Quine, Willard Van Orman. *From a Logical Point of View.* 2nd ed. rev. Cambridge, Mass.: Harvard University Press, 1961. (C, D, L)

————. *Methods of Logic.* 2nd ed. rev. New York: Henry Holt, 1959. (L)

————. *Word and Object.* New York: Wiley, 1960. (C, D, E, L, M)

————, and J. S. Ullian. *The Web of Belief.* New York: Random House, 1970. (C, E, F)

Rachels, James (ed.). *Moral Problems.* New York: Harper & Row, 1971. (2nd ed., 1975.) (A, G, O)

Rader, Melvin. *A Modern Book of Esthetics.* 3rd ed. rev. New York: Holt, Rinehart and Winston, 1960. (A, H)

Reichenbach, Hans. *Elements of Symbolic Logic.* New York: Free Press, 1966. (C, L)

Rorty, Amelie O. (ed.). MODERN STUDIES IN PHILOSOPHY. Garden City, N.Y.: Doubleday. (B)

Rorty, Richard (ed.). *The Linguistic Turn: Recent Essays in Philosophical Method.* Chicago: University of Chicago Press, 1967. (A)

Russell, Bertrand. *Introduction to Mathematical Philosophy.* London: George Allen & Unwin, 1919. (L)

————. *The Problems of Philosophy.* New York: Henry Holt, 1912. (D, E)
Paperback: New York: Oxford University Press, 1959 (Galaxy Books)

Ryle, Gilbert. *The Concept of Mind.* London: Hutchinson's University Library, 1949. (E, M)

————. *Dilemmas.* Cambridge: Cambridge University Press, 1954. (C, D, M)

Scheffler, Israel. *The Anatomy of Inquiry.* New York: Knopf, 1963. (E, F)

————. *Conditions of Knowledge.* Chicago: Scott, Foresman, 1965. (E)

Schilpp, Paul Arthur (ed.). THE LIBRARY OF LIVING PHILOSOPHERS. La Salle, Ill.: Open Court. (B)

Scriven, Michael. *Primary Philosophy.* New York: McGraw-Hill, 1966. (C, E, F, G, H)

————. *Reasoning.* New York: McGraw-Hill, 1976. (C, L)

Sellars, Wilfrid, and John Hospers (eds.). *Readings in Ethical Theory.* New York: Appleton-Century-Crofts, 1952. (A, G)

Shapere, Dudley (ed.). *Philosophical Problems of Natural Science.* London: Macmillan, 1965. (F, E)

Sidgwick, Henry. *Outlines of the History of Ethics.* 6th ed. London: Macmillan, 1954. (G, N)

Skyrms, Brian. *Choice and Chance: An Introduction to Inductive Logic.* Belmont, Calif.: Dickenson Press, 1966. (L, F, E)

Stevenson, Charles L. *Ethics and Language.* New Haven, Conn.: Yale University Press, 1944. (C, G)
Paperback: New Haven, Conn.: Yale University Press, 1960.

Strawson, P. F. *Individuals: An Essay in Descriptive Metaphysics.* London: Methuen, 1959. (C, D, M)

Suppes, Patrick. *Introduction to Logic.* Princeton, N.J.: Van Nostrand, 1957. (L)

————. *Axiomatic Set Theory.* New York: Van Nostrand, 1960. (L)
Paperback: New York: Dover, 1972.

Swartz, Robert (ed.). *Perceiving, Sensing, and Knowing.* Berkeley: University of California Press, 1977. (A, E)

Szasz, Thomas S., M.D. *Law, Liberty and Psychiatry.* New York: Macmillan, 1963. (E, F, G, I, M)

Toulmin, Stephen. *An Examination of the Place of Reason in Ethics.* Cambridge: Cambridge University Press, 1953. (F, G, J)

Paperback: Cambridge: Cambridge University Press, 1961.

Urmson, J. O. *Philosophical Analysis*. Oxford: Clarendon Press, 1958. (C, D, E, L, N)

Vetterling, Mary Braggin, *et al.* (eds.). *Feminism and Philosophy*. Totowa, N.J.: Littlefield, Adams, 1977. (A, G, O)

Vivas, Eliseo, and Murray Krieger (eds.). *The Problems of Aesthetics*. New York: Rinehart, 1953. (A, H)

Warnock, G. J. (ed.). OXFORD READINGS IN PHILOSOPHY (paperback series). London: Oxford University Press.

> Dworkin, Ronald M. (ed.). *The Philosophy of Law.*
>
> Feinberg, Joel (ed.). *Moral Concepts.*
>
> Gardiner, Patrick (ed.). *The Philosophy of History.*
>
> Glover, J. C. B. (ed.). *The Philosophy of Mind.*
>
> Griffiths, A. Phillips (ed.). *Knowledge and Belief.*
>
> Hintikka, Jaakko (ed.). *The Philosophy of Mathematics.*
>
> Linsky, Leonard (ed.). *Reference and Modality.*
>
> Mitchell, Basil (ed.). *The Philosophy of Religion.*
>
> Nidditch, P. H. (ed.). *The Philosophy of Science.*
>
> Osborne, Harold. *Aesthetics.*
>
> Parkinson, G. H. R. (ed.). *The Theory of Meaning.*
>
> Peters, R. S. (ed.). *The Philosophy of Education.*
>
> Quinton, Anthony (ed.). *Political Philosophy.*
>
> Ryan, Alan (ed.). *The Philosophy of Social Explanation.*
>
> Searle, J. R. (ed.). *The Philosophy of Language.*
>
> Seuren, Pieter A. M. (ed.). *Semantic Syntax.*
>
> Sosa, Ernest (ed.). *Causation and Conditionals.*
>
> Strawson, P. T. (ed.). *Philosophical Logic.*
>
> Swinburne, Richard (ed.). *The Justification of Induction.*
>
> Warnock, G. J. (ed.). *The Philosophy of Perception.*
>
> White, Alan R. (ed.). *The Philosophy of Action.*

Warnock, Mary. *Ethics Since 1900*. London: Oxford University Press, 1960. (G, N)

Wasserstrom, Richard Alan. *The Judicial Decision*. Stanford, Calif.: Stanford University Press, 1961. (I)

———— (ed.). *Today's Moral Problems*. New York: Macmillan, 1975. (A, G, O)

Weitz, Morris (ed.). *20th-Century Philosophy: The Analytic Tradition*. Readings in the History of Philosophy Series, Paul Edwards and Richard H. Popkin (eds.). New York: Free Press, 1966. (A)

Wittgenstein, Ludwig. *The Blue and Brown Books*. New York: Harper & Row, 1958. (C, E, M)

————. *Lectures and Conversations on Aesthetics, Psychology and Religious Belief*. Cyril Barrett (ed.). Berkeley: University of California Press, 1966. (C, E, H, J, M)

————. *Philosophical Investigations*. 3rd ed., G. E. M. Anscombe (tr.). New York: Macmillan, 1968. (C, D, E, F, G, H, L, M)

Wright, Georg Henrik von. *The Varieties of Goodness*. New York: Humanities Press, 1963. (G, M)

Index

About the Authors

Samuel Gorovitz is Professor of Philosophy and Chairman of the Philosophy Department at the University of Maryland. Previously, he taught at Case Western Reserve University, where he was Dean of Adelbert College. He received his B.S. degree from Massachusetts Institute of Technology and his Ph.D. degree from Stanford University.

Merrill Hintikka is Associate Professor of Philosophy at Florida State University. She has studied and taught at Mills College and at Stanford University.

Donald Provence is Professor of Philosophy at San Francisco State University, where he has taught since 1964. He is at present Chairman of the Philosophy Department.

Ron G. Williams is Assistant Professor of Philosophy at Colorado State University. He received his B.S. and M.S. degrees from the University of Colorado and his Ph.D. degree from Stanford University, where he served as instructor.